URGENT

ANDREAS WALTER

17 AND 84:
THE GODSCHA OF SONNEBERG

novum ◢ pro

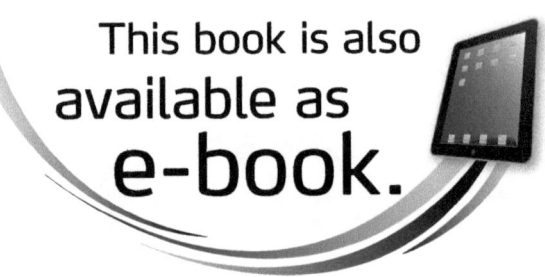

www.novumpublishing.com

© 2024 novum publishing

ISBN 978-3-99146-631-4
Translated from German:
Lingual Consultancy
Cover photo:
Jaromír Chalabala I Dreamstime.com
Cover design, layout & typesetting:
novum publishing

www.novumpublishing.com

Print product with financial
climate contribution
ClimatePartner.com/16547-2311-1001

INTRODUCTION

Saturday, December 7, 2013. Germany.

The grand charity gala "Ein Herz für Kinder" (A Heart for Children) is on TV in the evening.

Actress Jutta Speidel shares how she developed a four-year project with children in the Philippines 17 years ago. Host Johannes B. Kerner shifts the conversation to Veronica Ferres, a film star. During this exchange, he exclaims, "Only 17 days to go until Christmas!" Ferres shares an insight into her work with Roger Moore (James Bond actor in 1973). This live broadcast raised a staggering 16,386,291 euros in donations, or just under 17 million.

Everyone notices the recurring number 17. These ideas are of my own making. In nuce (in a nutshell) – 17 is the number of the Lord. This is the quintessence of my DU thesis (doctorate), which I defended nationwide in the form of letters in 1992. That was 3 years after the fall of the Berlin Wall, signifying the end of the Cold War.

In the field of architecture, the Golden Ratio is generally known as a harmonious numerical ratio. The numbers of the Lord reveal themselves especially in dynamic numbers: 17, its multiples 34 and 51, as well as 96, 69, 48. If that's too hot for you, we've still got the 84, i.e.: esteem-eight for human rights. Originating from the French Revolution of 1789, it proclaims that on Earth, one can do anything as long as it harms no other person. In matters of puncto puncti: This opens up a fascinating range of options.

There was a huge wave of enthusiasm in the Federal Republic of Germany (BRD). The news of this vision for the world spread through word of mouth. What has become of this, just one generation later? Mother Teresa of Calcutta, who received the Nobel Peace Prize in 1997, brought 50,000 souls to the Lord. Yet, she harbored doubts within. She longed for a sign from God. I received a letter of thanks from the Mother Teresa Children's Aid Fund. Second paragraph: "She taught for 17 years …"

The reason for the publication of my first letter was a plane crash in which 90 people had only 2 minutes left to live. Approximately 50% of the German population was of the opinion that this is all there is, with nothing more to come. The other half had a vague idea of heaven. That's why I'm placing the two letters at the beginning of the book (12 pages long in the original). I tell a complete story, and much has happened since then. Everything is authentic, with slight changes to the names of living persons. For almost 30 years, this ember of knowledge has been spreading and is now red-hot.

One thing you should know, however: When I tried to give my family physician, Dr. Heiter, a "Happy Retirement" card, I went to Müller's drugstore (opposite City Center Sonneberg), as they have a large selection of cards. There was a small group of about 5 customers waiting by the elevator. Suddenly, a man extended his arm, pointed at me and shouted, "You've done everything right!" He wore a rather puzzled expression and repeated, "Guys, that man there has done everything right!" They then entered the elevator. That was sometime in 2009. This book is for all denizens of Earth, regardless of their beliefs, for the children of this world, for the future of our planet Earth. The story unfolds gradually. Through my life story, I illustrate the impact of universal energy. We begin with a crescendo before the most unbelievable things happen, a drumroll before the furioso of the section "Free Energy for Everyone" with the subsections:

1. All the King's Horses
2. The 6th Kondratiev
3. Religion
4. Spatial Energy Technology Corona.

This brings a significant weight to my voice. Humanity is at a crossroads. Quo vadis domine? (Where are you going, Lord?)

Just as this introduction might come across, I too am a bit unpolished.

But this is my signature style! Any quirks in spelling are intentional.

Andreas Walter, May 2022

P.S.: In English, eight = estimate = estim-eight

BOOK ONE

17 AND 84
THE 2 LETTERS

Dear Sir or Madam,

This is a gift: a purely humorous piece of work, utterly devoid of any scientific merit – the facts have been dredged up from memory.

The tale of Jonne II, baptized: All of you who have been baptized in Christ have accepted Christ as your garment, celebrated the Lord's Supper – he carries Christ in his heart. Jonne II: The construction of an Archimedes-Hegel lever display case, solving pending questions. Archimedes: Eureka = "I have found it" (Law of Buoyancy).

The whole thing is an olive song inspired by the well-known stories of the Summbarch dialect poet Julius Heß Hegel: dialectical thinking. Behind it, Feuerbach: "Philosophers have so far only interpreted the world in various ways; the point is to change it" (Marx – dialectical materialism.) Hegel says: The world must be interpreted correctly. And mathematician Feuerbach lies behind it (circle: developed from a triangle through nine points). Nine is the number of perfection; 11 the number of humor. Hebel, Johann-Peter, the popular poet Hebel, "Give me a lever long enough and a fulcrum on which to place it, and I shall move the entire world." – thus spoke the inventor of the lever.

A Hegel lever, however, is a point lever: it pivots at a single point or over it up to here, with the spirit area depicted in the upper part of the box:

- the corpus area on the left: 5 fingers of the oath hand (also known as Jacob's Ladder)
- a compartment below, meant as a gate
- the Mentus area: 2 dolphins or 2 symbolic alpha waves emerge through laughter and joy in the two cerebral hemispheres
- then the "crib" with a calendar page from the day of constructing the box
- here, a peace pipe or house with a chimney + plume.

The small protruding piece of wood on the barometer symbolizes the next moment that will follow – here, the anima-animus realm = female-male soul realm coming from the cross or sword symbol.

The two frames, taken from a drawer, are connected with 2 Phillips screws, the center gap is created by inserting two washers.

A symbol of the time axis growing outwards = the 4th dimension – in the brain, a moment lasts about 3 sec, then the next one follows from that, represented by 3 subsequent grooves at the top edge of the box.

All parts were made merely using visual judgments; starting from the frame, only the sword hilt was measured at the end – 96 mm long, and at the bottom, the two vertical alpha parts are 60 and 52 mm long.

52 = 1/3 of 156 = height of the Cologne Cathedral. Continuing to the center: a tuning fork or sigma = sum sign, with the date of construction pyrographically etched.

To the left: God's sphere with the formula e to the power of 7 = 1,096, see the mathematical table – exactly 1,096.6.

7 – the number of faith, e = Euler's number = the base of natural logarithms. E also stands for Earth, technology, and science.

96: back-to-back = friendship/69: symbolic number of love.

So which questions are asked and answered?

1. Since the fall of the Berlin Wall in Germany, there has been peace on Earth. The arms race between capitalist and socialist world systems and the looming threat of a third world war have ended through a peaceful revolution. Inside is a box of European matches – 38 pieces with 12 stars in a circle – in one place the 8 peeks out of the 3, the whole thing is also a lift or Laozi pendulum, which, as is well known, shouldn't swing too far, on the right is the pulse-plus barometer of everyday life!
2. White cloth in the 7 mm drill hole, spirit anima-animus realm.
3. Geneticists are already assembling seeds, which have not germinated yet, however.
4. 4,000-year-old grains from ancient times sprout again.

All leading atomic physicists agree: In addition to the explored particles, there is a non-material "substance" that fills everything.

We know how a cell functions, but the inner driving force remains unknown.

Now, 300 witnesses from America – a television report – 45 near-death experiences, clinically dead individuals reporting:

- one sees the operating table from the outside and the surgical team's efforts to revive his heart
- another is struck by lightning in a phone booth
- one collapses in front of an X-ray screen and is clinically dead
- a personal interview with a woman who committed suicide

In summary: A figure made of light, a very beautiful, masculine figure, answers all your questions at the moment of their arising. Your entire life replays, all the positive, happy moments, even if they seemingly fade from memory during one's lifetime. For those who commit suicide, only the negative ones replay, hence the connection between the Cross, Anima, Animus, and Spiritus.

This brings us to the proposition: God also acts in everyday life (connection of everyday life = humus to spiritus = humor).

The following FACTUAL REPORT:

A Bavarian residing in Munich attempted to prove the Pythagorean theorem – "Number is the 'measure' of all things" – based on e raised to the power of 7.

He embarked on a bicycle tour from Munich towards Sonneberg.

First day of the tour: 260 km, one-hour delay in Ingolstadt. Overnight stop: Kleinziegentalfeld – Burgkunststadt.

Second day, Wednesday, 55 km (5 times 11), 17 h in total. He also had time to get a so-called "17-Marks" haircut.

At 11:11 a.m., he arrived at the city park "Bistro" in Sonneberg.

No one even knew that he would arrive on t h i s day, everyone had expected him on Thursday. He pondered, "What do I do now?" Meeting at 11:11 a.m.

- Jonne II without a prior appointment
- Lending of a leather saddle with the no. 92 28 11 30 29
- Subsequently, a visit to a store and the purchase of children's books for the home library, priced at around 186 marks = exactly the price of a taxi ride from Sonneberg to Weimar!

Witness: Summbarch cab driver Siegfried, known as the Nibelung!

q. e. d. – what does that mean?

Dictinary:

- Qui vive? – Whose side are you on? (French sentinel's challenge)
- Quod licet Iovi, non licet bovi – Gods may do what cattle may not
- Quipu: Incan writing device using knots
- Quirite: Honorary title of an ancient Roman citizen
- Quod erat demonstrandum = what was to be shown!

Look at your mouth: The area of OMM (Humus) has expanded to the area of ONN (Humor).

The first question:
How extensive is God's influence? Look at the double compartment in the center + time axis – infinite and eternal (a Hindu concept).
– This box received the "doubted and verified" seal!!

To continue:
– Le Bon: "To endow a man with faith is to multiply his strength tenfold!"

Praying and learning is also work (latest dictionary of philosophy, "Wörterbuch der Philosophie", Munich).
How should we encounter God?

– "Lucky Luke 11: Our Father ..."
– "Fear not!" Go into the stillness with the Lord, seek the "You," ask Jesus for help, and simply be in silence
– "Joy" is the greatest secret of Christians; it doubles when shared
– We will now proceed to Nostradamus (the most famous, recognized prophet of the modern age) with the e-to-the-power-of-7 key

e to the power of 7 = 1.096 =X,96: Whether something really happened, in reality, can only ever be confirmed after the fact.

X,96: "The faith that gives names to the seas will defeat the sect of Absallas' son, the sects mourn deeply, speaking Aleph and Eliph disdain for him." No additional explanation is provided.
Woe to those who sit where the scoffers sit!

X,48: "Coming from the ends of Europe, a multitude advances from Spain's background, drawing near to Lancias' bridges; a band strikes its great multitude" (Lancia near Rome).

X,44: "Against his own, a king from Blaye, is presently subjugating Liguria, Mammert, Dalmatia. The slain torment the king." Explanatory note: "Certainly, this refers to Henry II or the Fortunate, who will assume his rule as a world monarch in 1999. The wars he must fight have been imposed upon him by the Arabs or the leader of a large Arab empire. He must liberate significant parts of Western Europe from the Arabs."

X,46: Explanatory note: People thought of Adolf Hitler – (Austrian – a "foreigner"!), hence these shouts: They (those people) are exorcizing themselves! – who was appointed the government councilor by the B r u n s w i c k e r s in 1932, and who thereby obtained German citizenship and then became president of the German Reich.

But where is the Arab sect?
Now it will be exposed:
LEA SANDERS and her book "RAINBOWS OF YOUR AURA", Riverrun Press, 1987, will be presented.
Lea has had the God-given ability to see a person's aura (a light-emitting field that surrounds an individual) and their chakras (energy-light points in people) since she was a child (she's not the only one, but the best). She convincingly presents this in her book with examples and her life story.

To summarize: The soul of every person on our planet is about as old as the Stone Age. People purify the positive rays of their aura over multiple lifetimes and progress through the individual chakras toward the light: Lea sees this when she looks at people.
90% are on the cusp of universal love and they work hard. She suggests entrusting God with the care of your soul now to prepare for the afterlife.

She says: "The aura of Jesus is white with gray stripes."

And so the "omm" of the faiths of the eastern hemisphere (Yogis – Kundalini, Hinduists – Faith in God, Buddhists) would be extended to the "onn."

But what about the Mohammedans? They worship a god fatalistically, have no concerns for what comes after them, and see paradise on Earth in material things. There is no "hereafter" for them. They love things and use people.

A distinction should be made between the Arab people and the Arab way of thinking.

Three Arabic counterarguments and an additional argument:

- Car + environmental damage caused by production: the price is in fact 80,000 D-Mark, not 20,000 DM.
- Gasoline + environmental damage due to combustion: the price is in fact 5.00 DM/liter, not 1.50.
- Cars kill trees/+ people spend half of their time working for their cars.

The Finger of God, Luke 11, 20.

Latest research results (TV): Ozone layer already 15% damaged/ +10% damage per decade. It takes 20 years for CFC to reach the top – the immediate conclusion: max. 35% damage: close to the limit/now we can continue debating back and forth for another 10 years along the line of: We may be clean, but will India and China play along, then damage will reach 45% = ozone hole = the tipping point for the oceans' plankton in 2020!!!!

It's 12 o'clock on all environmental fronts. Either we all act now and the crisis is resolved by 1999, or there's no turning back after 2020!

A sign: Professor Rosin of Scharffenberg replaced CFCs with HCs in refrigeration technology (= price = energy = propane and butane is available at every third-world gas station).

Are you from Braunschweig? Do you have children? No comment on Braun?

Christian love of one's neighbor – "...love thy neighbor as thyself." – yes, most people love themselves, but what does "and" mean? It's true, "thyself" is in second place!

Near "Aleph" in the dictionary, it says, "The die is cast."

The cradle of humanity is in Africa; all languages have a common root.

Today's humans differ in only five genes, which primarily determine skin color.

Conclusion: Conference on Maastricht 51 to 48 = 3 x17, Liberty, Equality, Fraternity – 17.17 (John: "Your word is truth" + Luke 11: "Our Father ...", Christian charity as the basis).

Socialism/Communism supplies the idea of a material paradise on Earth, but technology without faith ... By 2020, we want solar technology and high eroticism based on e to the power of 7!

Le Bon: This writing was given to 79 cities in Germany; read, learn, share. Please distribute to the Chairperson of the County Office, Editor-in-Chief of the local newspaper, Church Leader, Mayor, and Main Railway Station Supervisor – Display James 4:17: "Whoever knows the right thing to do and fails to do it, for him, it is sin."

2 Cor 1:24: "Not that we lord it over your faith, but we work with you for your joy." Thank you!

Distribution: handwritten copy to 78 cities, 5 copies each, spiritual double reversal, faith and knowledge March 31. March – 1993.

The Battle for Water:

And this is Master Serious and Psychological Strain and not satire!!! Psalm 144:9: "I will sing a new song to you, my God, on the ten-stringed lyre I will make music to you."

The Battle for Water:

In addition to 30 million tons of gas waste over Germany's airspace, another 30 million tons of nitrogen oxides from car exhausts enter our atmosphere every year! (Acid rain – dissolution of heavy metals in the soil – groundwater becomes undrinkable.)

In many parts of the Rockies (USA – gold miners – mine dumps), drinking water is more precious than gold.

In Bavaria, deep wells already reach 400 to 600 meters into the groundwater. There is a significant difference: health-promoting spring water versus filtered/treated wastewater.

During the "Thalidomide trial," the judiciary failed to establish the direct causal relationship between Thalidomide and the damage it caused (in individual cases, it could have been another substance). However, anyone who administers Thalidomide today clearly causes harm because, if it were not the case, pregnant women would still be taking it!

Freedom of the People:

"Liberty consists in being able to do anything that does not harm others" Article IV of the Declaration of the Rights of Man and of the Citizen (1789). People who starve to death (40,000 every hour) cannot think!!

Nigeria: 95% of income comes from oil – the population has doubled to 100 million in the last 20 years – desertification = human-accelerated/natural desert spread – in northern Nigeria, the fight for water sources has already begun! So when will the pope finally build his no-chéri-(condom)-yes-factory?

Dictionary: "condom, noun" – top of the mornin' to you, Mr. Pope – don't you know that condoms are used in the missionary position too?

This was your "Tina Turner Air Mail", your hottest love spot!

Which brings us to the Rio summit: 5000 civilized specialists polluted the bay of Rio (massive death of fish) and left their IOUs where they still are today!!!!

Is your water still flowing?

German TV – the topic is alcohol = a quick phone poll: 61% of viewers were in favor of no alcohol in road traffic!! And everyone should set an example! Bonn: the debate goes back and forth "0.08 – 0.05% BAC" Clearly, the parties have widely deviated from the population structure in their respective sociological composition (financiers in the background). Creepy Pants Ltd (company) has known for 10 years already that the current energy concept is a dead end: 2,000 injured parties already and total damage of 20 billion marks. Anyone who continues down this road is a criminal.

8 – 4 (APPRECI-EIGHT HUMAN RIGHT 4)!!

You can usually experience the Cancellor in the Cancel-ory! Now he's got 48 hours for his bike – train discount card – blue jeans and GDR young pioneer's neckerchief! Or will it take a sixth-grader to say, "Hey Helmut, you've screwed my future on Earth!" When will the Cancellor finally start a Diamond Diet, in order to make it to those 4 hours of work at night that he has been depriving the nation of so far?

Note:

Wheels on the inside = training bike, bicycle, train, ship. Wheels on the outside = wheelchair – car – airplane

Mr. C.! You can work 25 hours a day like Hercules. If you can't do that without a car, all your work is pointless!

Your motto is likely "80 million Germans have cars – 1 billion Chinese build cars."

The capital = 10,000 financiers ...a handful of taste buds rule 10 billion thinking cells! C. snatches 10,000 marks per month from his fellow citizens and delivers nothing!!! (theft = to snatch, see the dictionary!)

Have you ever heard of the General's View? Council of the Hussar of the Neisse (J. P. Hebel): "There are deeds that must be answered for before God!!!" The good truth is not enough for some politicians, therefore the entirety and in full force.

The average salary of a "West" German is 5,000 DM per month, and Helmut is not even able to organize soup kitchens for the poor (they existed in 1848)!

Indigenous people think up to the 7th link and not about party positions! Recognize: You just don't have a tiger in the tank, but on your chest!

In 1996, interest took one in five marks! Mr. C, your legs come with strong bones: with rods, shafts, and heads, so you're an "Otto" engine if you can s i n g! Let the sparks fly!!

Get the power of black "PAN" T "HERS". 2 x 17 cats are incorruptible: the highway is the modern automic bomb.

Just imagine Helmut as the man with the 2 hats (stacked)! What a commotion there would be! C.'s question: "Isn't it rather complicated to implement?" "Nothing is easy the first time!"

Test question: "Why does the gardener wear a hat?" "So you don't have to press his eyelids shut after he falls off his bike!"

Here's one more question: What's the difference between doubt and trout? "Let's give it a shot!" "You passed! Any more questions? Quessssssstions?"

"What is the Diamond Diet?" "Harvey and Marylin Diamond."

4 million books sold in the U.S. – the same level as Galileo Galilei: The earth orbits the sun, in summary: essential energies move freely in all body cells and are used where people need them first – an infinite number of new possibilities for nutrition, also, as is tradition, a revolution in the field of eroticism – harmony in the partnership, 6 – school leaving examinations starting in 5th grade (books from Bathe Yourself Healthy to Navel Gazing).

Fight against the "slacker's heart" – 15 minutes of preventive measures during work hours! Get the power of the Black Panther! 141 Chinese people pictured laughing on a bike, "'Diamond' is the only way for me."

"Becker bakeries bake bread for charities like 'Brot für die Welt'" (by comparison: Earth can absorb 2 liters of oil per person per day – Germany consumes 12 liters of oil per person per day). Saarbrucken Public Utilities: Financing of the new e-technology (given to the consumer) using saved electricity!!! The energy transition is the rehearsal run for humanity's incarnation. Dolphins are the humans of the seas!

For children and adults: Offer two things – let them take one, for the other hit them on the fingers! Every human has 10 billion thinking brain cells, that's enough to speak 70 languages fluently!!!

Sex – guide, the first basic thought: the human brain is the largest sexual organ, next comes the entire skin, only then followed by the vagina – penis – clitoris – prostate. Get the 5 forms of energy to flow freely within you! Work on your aura! Thank you for decades of friendship of the SOS Children's Villages!

Space for dedication: "When one embarks on a journey!"

Bridge   Bridge

Bear Ye One Another's
Burden
Stephen Stich 96
Logbook: October 17, 1992 = soul inside
IOKI "2040" "Pull Over!!!!"

L – A – S – T SOLAR-LIGHT-POWeeR

LONDON

UNITED KINGDOM
QUEEN ELIZABETH

Sum 4

"The sun is the cot flower of our universe in the shining cot of the Lord 'Festus' of our Lord Yahweh, His Son Jesus."

RAINBOW BRAND
Merlin M. Moser

The "jellyfish" sails through the sea, so that you may all love and neck each other.

BOOK TWO

The Godscha of Sonneberg

The following biographical anecdotes are essential for a better understanding.

Carry on please!

1984
Eyes open. Where was I? I was lying in a bed, wearing a white hospital gown. There was a big window to my right, I could see trees. A rack with a towel stood to my left – was I in heaven? I had an IV dripping into my left forearm. Silence. What had happened? That's when it hit me: I had killed myself, then I blacked out! I was a medical student, in my 4th year, at the Medical Academy in Erfurt. Behind a screen, a woman in street clothes was sitting on a bed reading a book. Further beds were empty. I knew the ward from the night watch: intensive care in the surgical clinic. The attending physician checked on me. I asked him, "Are we friends?" What had actually happened?

After the summer term, I had experimented with autogenic training, back home in Sonneberg. In a book I had read: The subconscious mind has 10 times the capacity of the conscious mind. Consciousness determines the subconscious, and what had struck me? GDR: According to plan, the standard of living was supposed to get better and better – that was the message on replay everywhere. But everything just got worse and worse. Buildings were crumbling, roads were deteriorating. There was a 15-year wait for a "Trabant" car. The number of applications to leave for West Germany rose steadily. Environmental damage, air pollution, an economy of scarcity. The government and the media praised socialism, but the opposite was true! There was a gap here: a phase shift by the factor of pi, halfway between consciousness and the subconscious. I reviewed my discovery. It was the "Wave at Loose Ends" principle, as I had learned from the physics teacher Donnerberg.

The clash between the global capitalist and socialist systems was the order of the day. Instead of world peace, we got rearmament and the threat of nuclear war. I continued to work with suggestion and self-hypnosis. A tipping point was needed, a revolution. The subconscious takes the lead with everyone, and I was one of the first. Sleeping soundly was thus a thing of the past. I had to go to Erfurt. I took an early train. Suddenly I had lots of new ideas and saw the connections. Once I arrived, I took the streetcar to the children's hospital. I went to see Professor Vierring, whom I knew back from my diploma thesis. She was in her office. I looked at her and said, "To see people like this everywhere ...!" and burst into tears.

An ambulance then took me to the psychiatric outpatient clinic. I had a constant torrent of words, thoughts were racing in my mind. A doctor questioned me for an hour, "What's wrong with you?" But I wasn't allowed to reveal anything!

They took me to barracks with a wooden door. Welcome to the closed ward of the psychiatry unit! There were three other patients in the room, apparently with the same status. So things are in motion and the first ones are being locked away! Young nurses kept coming and asking, "Do you hear voices?"

That's when my father and my younger brother Bert showed up. They had come with an ETZ 250 ccm motorcycle from Sonneberg, about 56 miles away. Horror was written all over their faces. You won't get me! I pulled my Swiss army knife from my red travel bag. The window latches had screws on the inside. I unscrewed it with my screwdriver, climbed out and was gone!

There was no way I could stand another minute in that monkey's cage. I walked down the street in a westerly direction, asked a man washing his car, "Could you drive me to Sonneberg?" He turned me down.

I continued along a field, then along a country road to Nordhausen. I spotted a sandbox. You won't get me. I knelt down, felt the apex beat of my heart, thought my last ten thoughts. "... Check your grandmother's watch!" and then I pushed my knife's biggest blade deep into my chest, through my shirt, all the way. But it didn't work! Better try again! On my knees, I pushed the blade into the navel area all the way into my abdomen! Had I severed the aorta? I felt the cutting edge against my spine. But there was something there – I was not meant to die! And so I realized: I have to go back and do it my way! The knife came out. An unprecedented feeling of joy flowed through me.

And that's when the cop car pulled up ... I handed over my weapon. "I need to return to the clinic!" And I have no more memory from that point on. The OR. Anesthesia. Retrograde amnesia. The surgeons spoke of "artificial shocks." Nothing had been injured!

Intensive care. I stared into the mirror above the sink. I had bright eyes, shiny hair, looked like "blossoming life." Full of energy! At night, the nurses gave me a notebook to write in. They cried. Early on, a "doctor pal" came around with a shot – tetanus, exactly 10 years had passed. They came with an X-ray machine, radiated my abdomen (testicles). The rounds: "That's him, the one!" His Magnificence Usbeck, senior professor, patted around my belly and briefly glanced at my face. No visitors were allowed, I was very upset, hardly slept. After a week, I returned to my barracks with a large scar down my stomach.

Twin room, bathrobe. I had the whole day to think about what was to become of me. They lathered me up with haloperidol. Severely depressed. I befriended my roommate. We went through the front part of the barracks (open ward) through the door into the park. I only slept until 4 a.m. and suffered from tormenting thoughts. After four weeks, they let me go home on a Friday after rounds. I had 5 minutes to change trains in Arnstadt. Then I continued towards Saalfeld through the Thuringian Forest to Sonneberg. I read stories about the "olives" on the train.

Sonneberg originals in the Franconian dialect. That gave me a lot of strength, more on that later.

I then took a bath on Saturdays. I felt like my mind wasn't fully there.

Then something extraordinary happened: for an entire hour, only happy moments passed through my room. So I underwent this "therapy" twice a day from then on. I then received a second roommate – Frank from the theater. We went into town, visited Katrin König, such a theater kitten. They tried to transfer me to the 5th academic year. Lecturer Serpel, my physician, gave a lecture on the six causes of suicide. They all applied. Well why don't you just drop dead – I'm not going to kill myself!
My diagnosis: schizophrenia!

After 20 weeks, the matter of retiring came up. My psychiatrist to my father, "Take him home, there's nothing more we can do for him here!"

So what were the happy moments? In chronological order: I was born in the summer of 1958 in Sonneberg, Thuringia. My father worked as a ward nurse on a septic ward. My mother was a trained nurse. My brother "Volt" was two years younger than me, and brother Bert was three years younger. We lived in the alley "Am Stadtpark". There was a playground right across the way. My mother didn't work for ten years until we were all in school.
Schonni W., a friend of mine, did not attend kindergarten either. I built castles in the sandbox using moist and dry sand. Every couple of days, kids would suddenly appear in the park.
I used to get fresh milk from the specialty store with a gallon jug. I had a wooden car and a pedal scooter. We would put hot bricks in our beds in winter and the laundry would freeze. My parents gave me a book with the ten numbers and pictures.
One day Schonni showed up with a new friend and they beat me up. My two brothers came out of the house, watched it all, those two little imps! One day there was a kids' festival at the

park. They were playing "Duck, duck, goose!" Before I knew it, I was the goose and lost. And I was so embarrassed, never again!

My first day of school was on a Saturday and I had a lot of wood shavings in the candy cone they give you. On Monday I then went to the "Geschwister-Scholl" school right next to the park. My teacher Müller explained, "We write towards the margin!" When I turned the first page of my notebook, the margin was on the left. So then I wrote from right to left. The teacher grabbed me by the head and lifted me right off the bench ...

I had eye surgery in Erfurt because I couldn't adjust my spatial vision. One side of my glasses was taped shut. My parents would replace the tape. They'd ask me, "So which lens was taped off?" The first important question of my life! They operated on the left – that's the sick eye – tape! What a life-defining stroke, perfectly "wrong!" Did HE do that?

I was always tired in the 1st grade. Then we got a young teacher, Ms. Melbus, and things started looking up! I read fairy tales and animal books. We moved to a third-floor apartment on Juttaplatz square. There was an assembly on the last day of second grade. It was my birthday and the sun was shining. The principal handed me the book "Die fröhliche Minute" (The Merry Minute).

I shared a room with my brother Volt. School was not very far away. At night I'd hold my stuffed animals in my arms: bear – strong, lion – brave, giraffe has a great, wide view. In the mornings after waking up, I'd still see images flickering on my inner screen: castles, palaces, secret passages, princesses.

I was in a choir class. They kicked me out after a few rehearsals. We had a garden at Schönberg, near the forest house. We spent a lot of time there. We had the biggest cherry tree of the whole compound. A full tree, 23 feet tall. We learned to climb. There was also a shed. We had a rabbit hutch, even chickens for a time. Father slaughtered them himself for our Sunday roast every six weeks.

I collected stamps, mosaic booklets and built castles using plywood. Sunday morning I went out and collected plants (plant identification book).

My mother was from Römhild, 7 miles from Hildburghausen, which you could reach in an hour by train. We were invited to the Römhild farm every year for a few days. That's where I learned to ride a bike and to swim at the public pool. In 6th grade, I went on adventures at Hasenthal summer camp. Near the end of 7th grade I spent four weeks in the Pioneer Republic Werbellinsee outside Berlin. In the 8th grade I had my Youth initiation (Jugendweihe) civil confirmation ceremony. Then a trip with our parallel class was announced, and we stayed in a youth hostel in Berlin. I was the goalkeeper in Mr. Fiedler's handball team. My dream was to become a magician or an architect. At school, sitting on the bench next to me, was Chris, the daughter of a music teacher. I attended Hermann Pistor high school in the 9th grade. A Mr. Bischoff founded a judo club there ... In 10th grade, I scored the full 40 points at our district-level Mathematical Olympiad.

My brother Bert was cut from a different cloth; he never learned Russian. He had one entry that said: "Bert secretly smokes in the city park!" He also once placed incense candles under the school chairs. Principal Grund issued him a reprimand, saying "we narrowly avoided a school fire!"

10th grade exams: oral test in Russian, civics, astronomy. In astronomy I got a B, I had misspelled "Erdabplattung" (earth flattening) with a soft b!

We moved into a house in the upper town during the following summer vacation. My parents had bought it; it was a real fixer-upper in need of repair. Only the roof and the tiled stove were still in order. Architect Malsch made the designs and the plan to get the materials approved. My father and we three brothers also spent a week in the woods. The forester had marked trees for us by the Gunnersbach brook near Röthenquelle. We headed out early with an old crosscut saw. We had no car. Our bricklayer

Fritz Götz had given brother Volt a used RT 125. The timber was cut to size at the "Bubi" sawmill in Köppelsdorf.
In the 11th grade, they wanted to transfer me to Halle for a preparatory year to study medicine in Russia. My health certificate noted my weak eyesight. Russia said, "Nyet!" (No). That was a huge stroke of luck, life-changing!

Teacher Kegel gave a surprise test in chemistry, there was one question I didn't know. Applying for medicine with a B in chemistry, that wouldn't do. Suddenly, I saw orange before my eyes, and the formula came to me! That was HIM. Study in Erfurt or Jena? I thought about it for three minutes, then I picked Erfurt. If I had known that the first two years were to be spent in Leipzig, I would have chosen Jena. But my choice was the right one. I originally wanted to attend drawing class, but Doc Räder summoned me to join music class and choir! That was a real challenge! I read a chess book and internalized the thinking strategies of the last ten world champions. My brother Volt also joined the judo club.

French elective class, monument of a soldier in Paris, "Merde!", "Shit!" In the math specials camp in Ilmenau, I played Skat "Green without eleven trumps" and won with 61 points! I ate ten dumplings every Sunday! In the music exam, I sang the song "Am Brunnen vor dem Tore"! I couldn't answer the question in civics class – I got a B! In the oral math exam, I had to derive the complete integral.

Great-grandfather Frieder from Neuenbau had four sons, all of whom perished in the World War. His motto: "Blessed is he who has kept one thing in the struggle of life, his sense of humor!" My grandfather still managed to produce two sets of twins. Uncle Rolf found his happiness in Westphalia; the family counts ten grandchildren!

In preparation for medical school, I worked for two months at the district hospital on the Surgical Ward 3, Men. Anyone who did not go to the army for 3 years had to complete a full year.

So I gained my first experience in workflows and patient care. I traveled to Erfurt to enroll and register in the matriculation book – university no. 4848 of the academy!

I had an appointment at the military district office. The officer asked what I would like to do. "Medic!" "Those are all taken already, how about a quartermaster? You're good at math, right?" The quartermaster is the professional non-commissioned officer who oversees the regiment's pantry. And what happens when something is wrong with the food? I replied, "I won't do that!" We agreed on bridge-building pioneers, six months at the NCO school Eilenburg (east of Leipzig). I had flipped another switch! My service began on November 1, 1977. I traveled there the previous evening, dozed off in the train station at night, and started my army life at 6 a.m. in the barracks the next morning! We were kept busy and drilled around the clock, everything was planned out. There were about 20 comrades in one room. Assault course and a 1.9-mile run, god awful. I was the only one with a red bag. Could I take it along on leave? The platoon leader said, "That's a dark brown bag in my eyes!" In our field camp, we practiced with pontoons and got our boating license. We were also trained as explosives experts ... I ended up at Ponton-Dessau north of Leipzig, the bridge-building regiment. I was very unhappy about this job in the 3rd Company. The battalion commander Hofmann ordered me and two other NCOs to join him. He asked Ulrich and Fritsch, "How about becoming a reconnaissance officer?" They declined. I accepted. Independent group leader in the squadron, I was saved in the nick of time (HIM)! I had an eight-wheeled amphibious combat vehicle with a driver. Three reservists rowed the dinghy across the river, holding the measuring rod, and I looked through the level – river width! Ten 3-month reservists. The longest bridge: 350 yards, over the Elbe.

There is so much more I could share. Leave at Lake Scharmützel with secretaries in training. 1096 days for world peace!

October 30, 1980. Finished! Never again will I do something I don't want to do.

We left the barracks before 6 a.m., and I was in Sonneberg by noon. The following Monday we left early for Leipzig. Student dorm on Nürnberger Strasse 48, across from the Bayerischer Bahnhof station. Four-man room with the number 205. Ulli, Roche, and Ecke (a stomatologist) were there, a happy crew. 26 was my seminar group. The lectures were just getting started. I can't explain an entire physics program at Karl Marx University here! Every day we studied until 10 p.m. I drove home every 2 weeks. Studying didn't come easily to me. The lecture rooms were just off Liebigstrasse around the corner. The cafeteria was located in the university high-rise. Students tossed their expired meal tickets on a table. I collected them. The color, the date, and in small type the month! Using this trick, I always had two lunches! We also learned Russian, English, and Latin. I became friends with Linda, a stunning blonde. After the 1st year exams, we worked in the clinics for three weeks without pay. A head nurse picked me, and I ended up in the eye clinic, ward three. Linda injured her foot on the bottom step of the dorm stairs and was taken home (HIM). Things didn't work out for us.

I took my motorcycle test in Sonneberg and bought an ETZ 250 cc in a shop. We took anatomy classes in the 2nd year. The round lecture hall accommodated about 500 students. The dissecting room was right next door. Professor Leutert honed my scalpel! He had also written the textbook. We had ten exams, worked with microscopes using histological preparations. Biochemistry, physiology, and embryology were other subjects. But the course on probability and statistics was what I enjoyed the most. With Rudi, I advanced to training leader in small-bore shooting. I completed my mandatory night shifts at the eye clinic, read the files. We went to Coffe Baum, Auerbach's Keller, and Andrea winked at me Over the Pentecost break, six other students from my seminar group and I went on a four-day Rennsteig hike with tents and sleeping bags. It was great!! The exams were tough. Roche dropped out. I had my impaired eye operated; the rectus internus was shortened by 1/4 inch (Prof. Hass, Senior Physician Haas). That'll make the girls run away!

A few days earlier, I had done some soul-searching and thought, "Dear God, if you exist and things go well with my eye, I'll go to church – and clean up!" I was very surprised; that last part was not my own thought. That was my "deal" with God!

3rd year of studies in Erfurt, Medical Academy. I was assigned a triple room in a self-contained apartment with a kitchen and bathroom. I felt like we could use a table and perhaps a radio. So I found an ad for a house clearance in the newspaper. I took the streetcar to South-Erfurt and then walked. Suddenly I saw a note on the door of a house: "For sale: Table with padded chairs!" I made a deal with the owner. Got me a cart and pushed the set across town for two hours. Then I also got a tube radio. I was deeply in love with Conny D.

I went to a competition in Rostock with Dr. Mittag's judo club. Helga gave me a shelf for the radio ... Pathology exams: Tissue specimens – caseated lymph node and appendix. Pharmacology with Prof. Sprössig: Alkaloids! Microbiology was my favorite subject. I drank gin and tonic at the Engelsburg student club. I did my internship in Sonneberg with Dr. Forkel and Dr. Steinheisser. At the start of my 4th year, my fellow student Jürgen G. asked me to move into his triple room in the dorm on Donaustrasse and bring my "furniture" along. He was in Seminar Group 3, which organized the entire student carnival! Hennig was the organizer, and I was the creative mind. We put together two complete programs. I received praise from everyone.

In an hour-long conversation I presented why I did not want to become an officer with the reservists. Both professors were impressed. My friend Sylvia, a pediatric nurse, looked like the singer from "Roxette." Then I fell seriously ill with mumps and was bedridden for five weeks. I studied for my urology exam, got an A.

Two weeks later I began my psychiatric self-trials ...

In early January of 1985, I began working as an assistant nurse on the Surgery 3 ward in the Sonneberg District Hospital. Two shifts, weekend. Ward nurse Uschi. My mornings started at 6 a.m., while the late shift went until 10 p.m. Gisela, who helped out in the kitchen in the evenings, called out, "Finally, a smart guy!" I worked without thinking. Hang in there! Gisela's husband had built a house on Wehd. The intern Jens-Uwe was preparing for medical school. So I had made some friends.

One day I felt a sharp pain in my foot and I didn't know what to do. Dr. Öhler immediately put me on sick leave for six weeks. Depression. I figured the best thing would be to kill myself. Then I happened to read that you shouldn't do such a thing to your mother in the magazine "Soviet Woman." I also read about a student in the old naturopathy book by Brauchle. He had gone through the same thing. He cured himself and then went back to studying!

After a few months of work, I became severely depressed again. In the specialist hospital in Hildburghausen, they put me on a drip for 14 days. "Hydiphen makes life beautiful!" I never became depressed again!

The film "The Life and Work of the Schizophrenic Poet Alexander März" was on TV. Withdrawal from role expectations, social self-isolation, autism, hearing voices, stuttering thoughts and lapses, loss of intelligence with each episode!

In the spring of '86, I had a period of energy that was unbearable to those around me. Hildburghausen, closed ward, cells. The doctor said, "If our place was any nicer, we would be inundated with people!" Occupational therapy and nothing else.

I received a phone call from Erfurt in the summer. An exorcist had been exmatriculated. The new program director was familiar with my case, invited me to do my 5th academic year! Then came another call at 4 in the morning: my brother Bert had crossed the secured Hungarian-Austrian border with his wife while on vacation! Apparently he could no longer stand it in the GDR. He had been working as a dump truck driver in a quarry. Originally, he was supposed to become a criminalist. There he had to serve for a year and a half with the riot police in Meiningen. But he was aware of the political system. He was passionate about traveling and motor sports. He found a job with a camera company in Munich. We would likely never see him again in Sonneberg (arrest warrant).

On September 1, 1986, I started my 5th year of medical studies in Erfurt! I moved into a single room in the dormitory on Donaustrasse, a 5-minute walk from the clinic. Course outline: twelve exams in the spring (state exam). I had all the books. Early morning lectures, then a shower and a nap. Two hours of intensive self-study followed. I was in seminar group 6 – lots of nice people! And a great atmosphere! Roche had also returned, he had made it. Stephan, aka "Django", a stomatology student, drove me and Christiane (3rd year student) to Erfurt in his Trabant car on Sunday evening and back on Friday afternoon. Everyone was impressed by my originality. Heavy object = caution. One day, while glancing into the window of a bookstore on Anger Street, I saw a calendar with an image of an Amaryllis flower (named after a shepherdess from Greek Mythology). I went inside, didn't find anything, and left. That's when I ran into her: Katrin König (HIM). She was having suicidal thoughts. I cared for her, visiting her and helping to solve her problems. Death certificate seminar – two books, I studied all night! Top marks. Military medicine written exam, I recited everything to Karoline, but ended up with a D. I had a vegetarian dinner at the Domplatz square with Christiane, a visit to the theater.

End of the 9th semester. Practical training. 48 hours in the delivery room, gynecological clinic. A week before the exams, I suddenly experienced a lack of sleep and an explosion of energy. Things became very dramatic ... Roche and his friend Kufu were there when I ended up in the barracks of the closed ward. They strapped me to my bed, naked! After a few days, I was transferred to Hildburghausen for ten weeks. "He is cyclothymic!" (manic-depressive), a mood disorder!! Mania: delusions of grandeur, egotism, excessive spending, little sleep, great ideas, extreme creativity – all in phases, with no loss of intelligence. "We know nothing about this disease!" An endogenous psychosis. I inquired with Prof. Reichel about the diagnosis. He said, "Schizophrenic to abnormal personality development." In an instant, I realized my fate and said, "I just want to know, what can he (!) do?" The professor bent forward, opened his mouth wide, his eyes popped out! I never saw such a stunned face again. That was my experience in Erfurt.

In Sonneberg, I met up with the program director in town. He told me, "You did everything right!" My scholarship continued until August 31, 1987!

I looked for work – something with little physical strain and without night shifts. The agency: By pure chance (!!), there was an opening at the "Kulturwaren" wholesale warehouse in Sonneberg-Nord. Administration was on the Cuno-Hoffmeister-Strasse. They dealt in toys and arts and crafts, which were distributed throughout the entire district of Suhl. I was responsible for unloading the truck deliveries at the warehouse entrance along with two colleagues. We transported them to the various departments in the building using a pallet truck. Jochn did the paperwork, Fred was the Friday bratwurst griller. I became severely manic: six weeks inpatient care in Hildburghausen ...

The women at my workplace intrigued me. Jochn was off for six weeks with sciatica. Then I became manic again, but this time, I was able to manage it! I worked a reduced five-hour shift twice a week with Christiane. Mania can be a wonderful thing when you're not burdening anyone else.

My mother and I took a "trip to the West" in 1989. Her half-brother Ewald was celebrating his silver wedding anniversary. We met brother Bert and his wife, visited Munich for a few days ... In the summer of the same year, brother Volt, a civil engineer in Weimar, and his family invited me to Rheinsberg for a camping trip. On my train ride back on July 1, I read the New Testament.

I wanted to teach myself how to play the accordion ...

Then, in the fall, the Berlin Wall fell, Schabowski: "Without delay!" (November 11, 1989).

My parents and I explored all of Franconia on five-speed bikes ... In addition, my specialty was the forest run at Schönberg. The wholesale trade no longer had a future. I was kept on until late 1990 since they couldn't fire me due to my 50% disability. Then I'd sit around home, drinking tea, calling in sick to the employment agency and did "nothing" anymore! "We don't need you in production or retail!" My disability pension started in the fall of '91. Only then did I embark on my life's true work!

In November '91, I took a computer class at a night school. I didn't understand a thing. That's how much I had disintegrated.

"Right, let's proceed systematically!" At the public library I borrowed two books: Jesus exists/he does not exist. In the dictionary of philosophy I found the term "Theodicy = proof of God" and the phrase "Praying and learning is also work." Barbara and Birgit found me a yoga book on Kundalini power. The book "Kempo, the Art of Fighting" was very helpful for the development of various mental techniques. On February 29, 1992 (a leap year), I was invited to my nephew's birthday in Weimar. I didn't sleep for four days, experiencing a heightened manic state, feeling fit as a fiddle. I filled out a "Venture Passport" and developed a mantra: "Suntsusonnearthearthanthropopophilosopherjuh!" It meant: "Here I am with my program, God, reveal yourself!" I doubted whether I should go. That's when the phone rang, a sympathetic female voice: "OPERATOR HERE, PLEASE DO NOT WAIT!" That was sensational!!!!

It was early Saturday morning and the bus was not running yet, so I took a taxi. The lights were flickering in time with my mantra on my evening train back. Earlier at the Erfurt train station, the police and a female doctor had checked me. "You are epileptic and you're not on any medication!" I denied everything. I was back home in Sonneberg around midnight and enjoyed a lytic cocktail. Doctors Heiter and Öhler showed up early. Euphorically,

I recounted my partly Dadaistic experiences. I ended up in the HiBu Ward 10 with severe mixed psychosis. The station was undergoing remodeling, and there were only a few younger men there. Doctor Man-Gold drank a cup of tea with me. I felt like "Highlander" and told her the story of the old olive. I had won the "Blue Ribbon" and didn't let on that anything was amiss. Four weeks later, my father came by and organized my release. Now I was free!!

An entire year of manic work lay ahead of me. I was working on the great DU (Dr. universale). I adorned small miniature booklets with the formula e to the power of 7 = 1096, gave them away and then talked about the mathematics of God. The Summer Olympics were held in Barcelona: the numbers of the Lord!!! Had I found the "Philosopher's Stone?"

My room transformed into a magical chamber (equipment). The Bundesnachrichtendienst (German Intelligence Service) contacted me via the radio ... Dagmar's stationery store (on Schanzstrasse) was my contact point ...

At the time, brother Bert went on his bicycle tour: Munich-Sonneberg! Anja's parents invited me to the Malschenalm restaurant for the first day of school. Heike's family was in the outer room with little Michael – an explosion of humorous fireworks erupted from my "hawker's tray" for an hour. Then my childhood friend Schonni showed up. He was disabled, lived in a housing block in Wolkenrasen, had a pool table and a son in 5th grade. I began visiting him regularly on Sundays. Kai, a friend doing his vocational training and a very good player, was also there. This one time on my way there someone shouted out, "That's a hellux, he nevers sleeps at night!" Incredible! I had my first public appearance at Bless-Blouss-Cross (Blessberg- Blössenberg- Lauf) in Rauenstein. My outfit was very extravagant ...

I worked three times eight hours a day. Caught a bit of sleep on the couch. With five Tisercin, I was able to sleep through the night. At the Hubert Gädtke gallery, I bought a painting titled

"Sunday Joy" for 300 marks, painted by Annelie Schenke with watercolors.

I assisted Wolfgang Kuebart, the Toy Museum Archivist, with his presentation on the "Olive Stories." I built a type case and presented it to Gädke and Kuebert. At the hospital, I talked with Michael from Nigeria in English for two hours. "A man of 2 and 2 is 4!" In the evening, I planned to present the type case to the Baptist minister on Juttastrasse.

All night my mind was on repeat: "We know everything, you know everything!" I "dissociated," God showed up through a dialogue in my head. I perceived the Holy Spirit as a knocking in my left ear and Jesus in my right!!!! The type case appointment was an early one. The perfect A-Team! Four Christians listened to my story. Never again have I seen such glowing faces! The pastor said, "Nostradamus isn't our prophet, I will escort you outside!" So, what next? A tremendous voice called from Eichberg, "Well, come on!" So back home then ... "Kingdom of Heaven on Earth is a reality in the making!"

God tested me – I held a FIVE-DAY DIALOGUE PLEA with four times 20 minutes of sleep. And behold, it was good!!!! I partied with Jesus for six weeks. Incredible things on TV! Three-speed bicycle with down-friction hub gears ... I got myself color TV ...

Sundays, evangelic parish church. Development of a library, wanted to become an "andrologist." With Klaus Hess in the "Sumbarcher Loudn." Purchase of postcards. I lugged everything to Schonni for the "Fasching" carnival. Kai – chess: Checkmate in three moves, board rotated 90 degrees! Plane crash: publication of the 1st letter, handwritten! Wineshop owner Wein-Gebler recognized me and shouted, "Jonne II!" Dagmar's store was shut down. I also tutored Susanne, an 8th grade student, very good grades (lived in the neighborhood). I played pool with her every three or four days on a table that Schonni had given me. The German intelligence service announced on the radio early at 4 a.m.: "Is that a Norman closet? We've all got some congestion on our backs! 65 years and not a day older!" I often stopped by the Bacara coffee shop on Kemmleinshügel. After a strong sign from God, I published the letter "84." A "real miracle": On Sundays I used to go to Schonni, have some cake. Dagmar passed away after a short, serious illness.

My thoughts and the environment blended, it all became one, I drifted into social isolation. My parents didn't understand, I fed myself, had an electric hotplate in the room, even wanted to move out. I was more thither than hither. In the spring of 1993, I was invited to Susanne's youth dedication ceremony at the Frankenbaude inn. I ate nine dumplings. Susanne was interested in wrestling and followed the show "Parker Lewis Can't Lose!" on TV. I easily have another 1000 lines and thoughts to share about that manic year! But I'll keep it brief: complications arose!!!

(I had given the typesetting box and the original texts to the director of the toy museum, Dr. Hoffmann, for emergencies!) It started quite harmlessly, I suddenly heard voices in small noises. The day came when things became severe. I talked to a dripping roof gutter all night long. What was happening? I asked Jesus for a clue, wrote on a piece of paper: "The Sonneberg bell!" When I walked past houses, I could hear what the residents thought and vice versa!!! My thoughts radiated across the entire town. The word "Gotha" (go daily) became "Godscha" and I telepathized, "A Godscha is in the eye of a town's aura tower!" The people communicated. After work, my father would shout down the hallway, "This Godscha's really got it!" One day I kept "rustling" all the time. My mother on the phone: "We've got a Godscha in town, but he keeps rustling everything up!" I had to get out of this situation!!! Since I needed physical contact, I headed out and shook the hand of everyone I met. A roofing crew's radio loudly announced: "Andreas Walter is walking through town shaking everyone's hand!" Mrs. Lippmann and her spouse: "He is Godscha and runs Gotha!" This hell continued for four weeks!!! I turned to my parents and dined in the kitchen again. The voices resumed after a few weeks. Dr. Heiter – Loretam for sleep. Dr.

Öhler – Glianimon. The city, thank God, remained quiet. This happened a total of five times, always for four weeks. The Glianimon disrupted my vision and impaired my thinking! Stuttering thoughts, lapses, a blank mind. Had to lie down for two to three hours until the episode was over. Couldn't go into town in the afternoon and evening, otherwise it would start up again right away. Severe schizophrenia. I was burned out. I just couldn't carry on! I desperately had to get to Hibu or it was all over! Surprise: Hibu – a new clinic complex for 20 million German marks!!! All-day therapeutic treatment, the very best! I learned to deal with my visual impairments. In the summer of 1994, I had to go to Neuhaus am Rennsteig for an expert opinion.

I took the bus, suffered a massive visual impairment for five hours. Things unraveled quickly from there. Renewed hospitalization in the fall of '94. My medication: Fluanxol. Ten weeks of recovery ... Continued visual disturbances despite this, but only about once a week for an hour. I was also given the mood pill Tavor (as needed) and Zolpidem to sleep at night. I only ever left the house early in the day. Until 2002, I was muddling around in the swamps of schizophrenia. That's when I met Renate, who invited me to a support group. I met Tana there ... Throughout 2003, I tested all kinds of medications with Dr. Öhler until the highest dosage of Olanzapine proved successful. No more visual impairments and only minimal voices!!! I was mentally drained and completely isolated socially. So now I had to completely re-build, reinvent myself. In 2007, I became severely manic for six weeks and wrote a letter on the subject of "climate change." Olanzapine also held up during manic episodes! Outside the house I heard a loud voice: "If you don't write, we'll all go to hell!" After all, not everything was as simple as I had made it out to be. So let me present my piece on climate.

BOOK THREE

Remember:

17,17 – Your Word is Truth (the Bible: God Exists), 1992

    8-4 appreci-eight Human Right 4 (do not harm another human being), 1993.

    NEW in 2007, JONNE II – CLIMATE VISION 3 PAGES. PLUS President of the USA, George W. Bush (Mister B). Didn't you hear the hurricane trumpets of Jericho! 12 o'clock!!

I have watched Michael Moore's movie Fahrenheit 9/11 twice and do not understand why you were re-elected. You are a smart businessman – you sold the American people a war (Iraq) and they bought it! A pile of shark crap! Total cost: $2 billion per week and 3,000 U.S. troops killed. In your next life, you should be reincarnated in starving Africa! Mister B: "I don't believe in reincarnation, there's nothing about it in the Bible." So you're a black smoker?

Well, in 325 A.D., at the Council of Nicaea, the doctrine of reincarnation was first officially wiped from the Bible; in 535 A.D., at the Council of Constantinople, it was finally declared a heresy.

    Mister B: "Ok, what about planet Earth?" The patient wants to hear the truth, but the pleasant one, so let's give it to him! UN Climate Change Conference in Nairobi (Kenya), 6 calculation models: The Earth's temperature will rise by 1.8 to 6.4 degrees Celsius by the year 2100. Main climate gases: water vapor, methane, carbon dioxide (CO_2). Methane is 200 times more dangerous than CO_2 and is stored as methane hydrate in large quantities at the bottom of the world's oceans. If the ocean temperature rises by 3 degrees Celsius, this methane will be released – and that would spell the ultimate end for humanity's climate on Earth!

The CO_2 released by industry has already caused warming by 0.7 degrees Celsius. Furthermore, due to the polar ice caps melting, sea levels will rise by 23 inches by the year 2100 (complete melt 164 ft). The cities on the coasts and large river deltas are the first to be affected. The polar melt is a cura posterior (later concern). What matters now is global warming due to CO_2 emissions.

Mr. B: "Why are there multiple computer models?"

The population figure is difficult to forecast! Will there be 7 or 10 billion people? China is acting very prudently here: The one-child policy applies (5% global arable land, 10% world population). Earth is a planet of free will! The motto is: free speech! There are always several possibilities! 0.7 degrees + 1.8 degrees = 2.5 degrees would be just below the critical mark of a 3-degree Celsius increase! (Walter 2022, 2015 Paris Agreement – 195 states: An increase of 1.5 degrees is just manageable, 1.1 degrees Celsius increase has already been reached!).

Mister B: "But what can we do?" Nicolas Stern, former head of the UN World Bank, has calculated: If we don't invest 1% of the world's gross national product now, we'll soon have to pay 20 times that. What does a storm (Kyrill), flood (Elbe, Oder) cost per year in Germany? 3 billion euros divided by 100 million citizens results in 30 euros per citizen now, soon that will be 20-fold (600 euros per year and citizen). That would be the price of CO_2 in Germany (10.2 tons per year), so 1 ton is roughly 60 euros!

Mister B: "I've been quoted a price of 67 euros per ton of CO_2 from a different source." How about this offer: 69 euros per ton of CO_2?

Mister B: "Deal, how do we fund it?"

First off: 1 pound of carbon produces roughly 1.64 pounds of CO_2. Second: 10.2 tons of CO_2 divided by 300 days = 66 pounds of CO_2 per day per citizen. This roughly corresponds to the consumption of 3 gallons of oil in Germany.

Third: 1 ton of CO_2 costs 69 euros in carbon dioxide tax = Earth tax calculation – the "EarStB" = Earth Stick B. You will notice very soon which products increase in price due to their unfavorable CO_2 balance. Initial financing: take out a small loan, buy 2 energy-saving light bulbs (6 times as expensive, 6 times as long-lasting as a normal light bulb, 1/5 power consumption, 3-year warranty, recyclable; 1 kWh at 16 cents), and get help from a home energy consultant (Nicolas Stern: 275 billion euros worldwide).

Dr. Angela Merkel, the German Chancellor and future President of the Council of Europe, has calculated that the accumulation of the World Bank's capital will take 3 years (democratic legislation worldwide). It's sufficient for the 12 most important CO_2 polluter countries (including Germany and the USA) to come to an agreement. Then China will jump on board as well! On average, this would mean 690 euros per year per citizen divided by 10 months, so about 70 euros per month! 50% savings are possible without any investment!!! (35 euros). Simply avoid anything that consumes energy and/or produces CO_2. Except: CO_2-neutral energy sources (wood, biogas, hydropower, wind, solar). Here's what everyone can do: lower your room temperature by 2°F – saving you 6% on heating costs (living rooms 65 degrees, bedrooms 60 degrees; use a room thermometer). After hot water, take a quick cold shower (toughens you up). Heating method according to Jean Pütz: one extra sweater/smart ventilation // smart washing/showering/bathing, more frequent vacations at home (balcony) // refrain from air travel/no imported fruit – eat more "sauerkraut" // meat consumption of 16 oz per week is sufficient // soup days, refrain from smoking (professional advice). For further savings with investments (approx. 35 euros per month!!) there's a whole slew of options: Buy more energy-saving light bulbs // replace stand-by circuits with multiple plug switches (eliminating 2 of the 17 nuclear power plants in Germany), modern solar cells – photovoltaics // solar collectors – hot water // decentralized energy supply // wood heating (pellets), geothermal heat // combined heat and power plants // biogas.

Hydrogen technology is humanity's ace up the sleeve! Dr. Ottmar Edenhofer has calculated that if we make use of all innovations, Earth's temperature (climate) will rise by 2 degrees Celsius (Paris 2015: warming of 1.5 degrees Celsius is just manageable!).

Further options: go on vacation by bus, train, boat. At home: modern windows and refrigerators/facade insulation with Styrofoam (1.5 inches = 15-inch brick wall)/interior insulation with vacuum panels (1 inch = 40 inches of Styrofoam)/roof and basement ceiling insulation (mineral or glass wool).

In urban settings, a 3-liter car is enough (you never conquer the countryside with a gas pedal, you do so with your foot pedal). No one needs to tighten their belt for these 35 euros per month. Just think of your insurance policies, building loan contracts and savings (households). The World Bank funnels most of it back into solar technology as subsidies. There is no better retirement plan than preserving Earth. An amount corresponding to 17 oz of oil consumption per person per day is transferred to developing countries (emissions trading), because the earth can cope with these 17 oz in the long term.

Mister B: "But what can I do, personally?" So 2 plus 2 is 4 and not 3 or 5. Take Michael Clair's advice to heart: 25% of the military budget for solar technology! Native Americans will consider up to the 7th generation when making a decision. Plant 1,000,000 trees (climate regulating, humus forming, counters desertification = devastation) like Mangari Maathai (Kenya: Green Belt movement since 1984, 3 million trees already). The next 100 years are at stake – and the minds of people is what it's about. Forget the nuclear age, there is no such thing as a safe atom (1 Castor = special container for radioactive waste has the radiating potential of 40 Hiroshima bombs).

A paradigm shift (a change in the way we think) towards the solar age! Get rid of the sonar bomb (sound): Whales and dolphins are special animals. Their brain hemispheres sleep in alternation. In summary: the centerpiece – an Earth tax (carbon tax) of 69 euros per ton of CO_2 produced (exception: CO_2-neutral energy sources).

Mister B: "What is the mission of the UN World Bank?" It finances the subsidies for solar technology and above all the program against overpopulation (highest savings potential) in developing countries (birth control pill, condom; 40 million suffer from AIDS), continued efforts to stop tropical deforestation (tipping the scales of the world climate – every tree counts!). Solar cooking is a global way out of the crisis: Dr. Seifert for 18 years, 15,000 parabolic solar stoves in 80 countries (1/3 of humanity affected, need: 200 million). The man who moves a mountain begins by carrying away small stones – Chinese proverb. In addition, the biodiversity of the world's oceans must be protected – dangers posed by overfishing (need 4 to 14 billion euros) – sustainable fishing, 1 million jobs. Nicolas Stern once again: Only a consistent rescue plan will help! 2.3 billion people live on a single dollar a day, 2 billion without electricity. With what it takes to progress from 99 to 100 in the industrialized countries, you can make it from 0 to 90 in the global south! At the moment, one half of humanity is still laughing at the expense of the other (there are 946 billionaires worldwide). A cost-neutral lunch costs 3.04 euro in Germany, but 50 cents worldwide. In the famine-ridden hell of Sudan it's only 33 cents. 36 million people starve every year! Dr. Angela Merkel stated, "Every citizen must be led to conscious action!" (CO_2 awareness/a feeling for one's own CO_2 belt). Taking environmental requirements into account, the economy first and foremost has to serve the people – and not the other way around!

UN report, part 3: Humanity still has a window of 13 years to implement the "Star" rescue plan, otherwise the disaster (the collapse) will ensue. Transport (by land, air, water) represents 21% of greenhouse gases in the 15 old EU member states. Of these, cars produce 10% (especially detrimental: cold starts and short drives). A flight from Munich to London produces 0.5 tons of CO_2 per person, Munich to Mallorca only 154 pounds – that's the same amount as a person in India produces during an entire year. We all know that you make just as much progress in your car whether you are going 110 or 80 mph. Environment

Minister Gabriel has calculated that a speed limit would save 5.6% in CO_2 emissions produced by driving – absolutely right! Mister B: "How much CO_2 does a 3-liter car produce per mile?" You do the calculation (key!): 1 pound of gasoline/diesel produces roughly 3 pounds of CO_2 b) a consumption of 3 pounds/100 miles corresponds to 0.50 ounces per mile. "How much more expensive will gasoline become?" Let's grab our abacus (ancient calculation device):

a) 69 euros per ton of CO_2

b) 5.6 oz of CO_2 per mile (3-liter car), 32000 oz per ton, 69 euros / 32000 x 5.6 = 0.012 cents per mile!

The hybrid (dual-fuel) engine was invented in Germany (using multiple fuels, including liquefied gas), but people missed the market launch! Despite increasing the engine power by 40% to 60% in recent years, they are now building racing cars with 14 ounces of CO_2/mile. So what is feasible? Smart diesel: max. 90 mph, 3.4 L per 60 miles. Emissions: 5 oz CO_2/mile! Japan builds the Toyota Prius: hybrid (gasoline-electric motor), 78 hp, 6 oz/mile. By comparison: the GDR's Trabant car had about 26 hp, max. 62 mph, 5 L of gasoline per 62 miles. Planned in 2008: The first German hybrid car/"Loremo": 1.5 L/60 miles (spec. feature: only half the weight of a mid-size car). Planned: Conversion of the vehicle tax from engine capacity to CO_2 emissions. (Toyota Prius 2 euros per year) – the point here too: The customer comes first! Think ecologically, economically, and globally!

Mister B. – more questions! "The Pope!" – There's simply no more room! Support the use of contraceptives around the world! (Most souls do not incarnate until the 5th month of pregnancy.) The Bible needs to be framed within its historical context. The next pope will have the chance to call himself Benedict the XVII. "Has Christ ever been resurrected?" – Yes, the Bible describes 9 cases of resurrection. "Which is correct, reincarnation or eternal life?" Is light a wave or a particle? They're both correct! Jesus shares bread, the Dalai Lama shares knowledge, and Buddha teaches 84,000 paths. "What does 69 stand for?" Also for Yin and Yang, the female-male principle of Chinese philosophy. "A marketing idea!" Dr. Hittich plants 10 trees for each customer's birthday! "Wood!" – Practically the perpetuum mobile of climate protection (plantations). "Biogas" – made from liquid manure or corn residues in Germany/Africa: ferns (Morocco). "Meat" – 3 pounds per week in Germany. Prof. Bankhofer: half a pound is enough! "Cattle" – generate a lot of the world's methane (greenhouse gas). "Genetic engineering" – you want to be better than God (rainforest reservoir)! "How was AIDS created?" – Humans ate the flesh of monkeys, who are immune! "Health" – introduce sugarleaf, stevia, rebaudiana into your diet! Would you board a plane that has a 1 in 7 chance of crashing? Every 7th smoker dies of lung cancer; 17 billion euros in damage in Germany.

END OF DISCUSSION

This text was created in the eye of the Lord. Therefore, it is free to use in any way. Feel free to copy and translate it! Inform important people! Be there when the spirit conquers matter!

Nicanor Perlas: "The heart of the revolution is the revolution of the heart."

Jonne II, April 8, 2007

This letter was sent to 100 city mayors in Germany. Zero responses, no reaction at all!
Earth is racing towards an abyss, everyone is carrying on as before. I was horrified, my heart, my life!

A severe anxiety disorder followed, then burnout, for 2 years. I distanced myself inwardly, withdrew into myself. No more chances and the certain death of the Earth's population before my eyes. But I had not lost my intuitive trust in God. Everything has already been invented, there's nothing new to come! I escaped into the world of music with my accordion (40 basses).

My 9-year-long journey of studying the Bible came to an end. I was also taken with the wealth of German folk songs. In 1847, Councilor of Commerce Fleischmann built the Villa Amalie near the Lutheran church. A descendant of his converted it into a private multi-generational house after the reunification of Germany. This Dr. Joachim Schede previously worked in the Ministry of Economics of the government in Bonn and Berlin. I joined a friendly group of senior singers in this villa starting in 2009. Together with Ms. Lieselotte Ross, we met every 4 weeks and would enjoy coffee and cake after our sessions. On Thursdays, there was an all-welcome regulars' table with Elke: drinks, cake, then a lecture, dinner (menu), 114 times.

The building accommodated a sewing workshop, woodworking shop, modeling, and toy design for children. The light was preserved there. In 2015, Dr. Schede and his wife Dr. Maria Schede passed away and the house was closed down.

The town of Sonneberg (Thuringia) was founded in 1349. Toy manufacturing developed there out of great poverty. With the coming of industrialization, toy production developed world-wide. In 1910, at the World Exhibition in Brussels, the monumental show group "Thuringian Fair" was presented. (It is now located in the Sonneberg Toy Museum.) Large American trading enterprises operated in town at the time. Hence the name: "World Toy Town". For 50 years, the first American consulate in Germany. Even during the 40 years of the GDR, all of Sonneberg worked in toy manufacturing – the most peaceful town in the world!

BOOK FOUR

All the King's Horses
Freie Energie für jeden Menschen

Quanten-Äther, Die Raumenergie wird nutzbar
Ulrich F. Sackstedt 2013
Raumenergie – Neue Energiequellen zum Nulltarif
Wilhelm Mohorn 2016
Forbidden Science
Richard Milton 1994
Der Geist in der Materie
Eckhard Kruse 2013
Perpetuum mobile – Die Geschichte eines Menschheitstraumes
Arthur W. J. G. Ord-Hume 2014
Energie aus dem Nichts
Jürgen Heinzerling 1995
Das Geheimnis ewiger Energie
Andreas von Retyi 2015
Energie ohne Ende
Andreas von Retyi 2013
Energie Harvesting, Energie aus der Umgebung
A. and I. Schneider, Achmed Khamas 19
Der Wassermotor
Adolf und Inge Schneider, Jose Vaesken Guillen 19
Die große Transformation in Technik und Bewusstsein
A. I. Schneider October 2020
Auf dem Weg in das Raumenergiezeitalter
Adolf and Inge Schneider 2020
Bahnbrechende Energietechnologien
DVD 2020 (Kongress)
Countdown
Mojib Latif 2022
Unsichtbare Welten

Armin Risi 2022
Breakthrough Power: How Quantum-leap New Energy Inventions Can Transform Our World
Jeane Manning, Joel Garbon 2012
Die Heureka-Maschine
Adolf and Inge Schneider 2017
Mit freier Energie gegen die Klimakatastrophe
Peter Lay 2007
Experimente mit dem Stirlingmotor
Ulrich E. Stempel 2014
Freie Energie – Oder warum fliegen UFOs?
Adolf and Inge Schneider 2014
Verschlusssache Antigravitationsantrieb
Paul A. La Violette 2010
Neue Experimente mit freier Energie
Ulrich E. Stempel 2015
Urschöpfungskraft und freie Energie
Anton Stangl 2009
Neue Energietechnologien
DVD Kopp-Verlag 2015
Raumenergie – Die unterdrückte Alternative zur Atomkraft
DVD, präsentiert von Prof. Dr. rer. nat. Claus Turtur
Der Quantum Energy Generator
Adolf and Inge Schneider 2014
Freie Energie für alle Menschen, Raumenergiemotor: Nachweis und Bau
Claus W. Turtur 2014
Verbotene Erfindungen, Energie aus dem "Nichts"
György Egely 2017
Metamorphose der Menschheit
Dieter Broers 2018
Denkt mit!
Harald Lesch 2021
Metahuman: Unleashing Your Infinite Potential
Deepak Chopra 2020
Be Angry! – Die Kraft der Wut kreativ nutzen

Dalai Lama 2019
Coronomics – Nach dem Corona-Schock: Neustart aus der Krise
Daniel Stelter 2020
Aus Liebe zu Deutschland – Ein Warnruf
Hamed Abdel-Samad 2020
Quantenphilosophie und Interwelt
Ulrich Warnke 2013
Cancer and the New Biology of Water
Thomas Cown 2020
Wir waren im Himmel – Nahtoderfahrungen in der Kindheit
P. M. H. Atwater 2020
Der Sieg des Abendlandes – Christentum und kapitalistische
Freiheit
Rodney Stark 2005
Manipulierte Gene – verdrehte Welt
Steven M. Druker 2015
Heilen mit Berührung – Streichen Sie den Stress weg!
Michelle Ebbin 2017
Das geheime Leben der Seele
Sabine Wery von Limont 2021
Unsterbliches Bewusstsein – Kontinuität des Selbst jenseits
vom Gehirn
Ervin Laszlo, Antony Peake 2016
Neun Tage Unendlichkeit (Eine außergewöhnliche Nahtoder-
fahrung)
Anke Evertz 2019
Quantenwelt
Lee Smolin 2019
Mensch, Erde! Wir könnten es so schön haben
Dr. Eckart von Hirschhausen 2021
Darm mit Charme
Giulia Enders 2016
Am Arsch vorbei geht auch ein Weg
Alexandra Reinwarth 2016
Psychische Erkrankungen anders behandeln
William J. Walsh 2016

Engelseelen, Wegbereiter
Zora Gienger 2017
Gesundsein
Louise L. Hay 2013
Geführte Selbsthypnose
Beate Blumrich 2016
Erinnerungen an den Himmel
Wayne W. Dyer 2016
Reichtum ohne Gier
Sahra Wagenknecht 2016
Wer regiert das Geld?
Paul Schreyer 2016
Die große Enteignung
Janne Jörg Kipp 2015
Die Welt verändern
Margot Käßmann, Heinrich Bedford-Strohm 2016
Die Zitronensaftkur
Tom Woloshyn 2015
Mach dich unbeliebt und glücklich
Diana Dreeßen 2014
Omas großes Gesundheitsbuch
Dr. Jörg Conradi
Die Wahrnehmungsfalle
David Icke 2016
Junge Seelen, alte Seelen
Varda Hasselmann 2016
Energieheilung
Ann Marie Chiasson 2013
Mathemagie für Durchblicker
Arthur Benjamin 2016
Die letzten Tage von Atlantis
Karin Tag 2016
Megawandel
Johannes Holey 2016
Hochsensibel, was tun?
Sylvia Harke 2016

Schutzengel und Co.
Martina Heise 2016
Om, die Ursprache der Seele
Shri Balaji Tambe 2016
Wie du deinen Partner änderst
Chuck Spezzano 2015
Kraftquelle Ahnen
Monnica Hackl 2016
Lobbykratie
Markus Balser 2016
Heilende Räume
Esther M. Sternberg 2011
Hand und Fuß, Quellen der Heilung
Friedrich Butzbach 2016
Das Geheimnis wahren Reichtums
Shakti Gawain 2004
Weizenwampe Detox
Dr. med. William Davis 2016
Die Homöopathie des Mondes
Susanne Dinkelmann 2013
Wunderwurzel Kurkuma
Dr. Jörg Conradi 2015
Drachensturm
Markus Gärtner 2015
Märchen und Sagen der Indianer Nordamerikas
Karl Knortz 2017
Bittere Pillen
Kurt Langbein 2017
Die geheime Kraft der Träume
Denise Linn 2013
Detox mit Yoga
Ann Trökes 2015
Die besseren Pillen
Kurt Allgeier 2017
Denkspiele
Ines Moser-Will

Leuchtende Chakren
Barbara Arzmüller 2016
Gesundbeten mit Heiligen
Monika Herz
Energiepflanzen im Haus
Eva Katharina Hoffmann 2009
Saat der Zerstörung
F. William Engdahl
Die ursprüngliche Lehre Christi
Daniel Meurois 2017
Das Leben macht Geschenke, die es als Probleme verpackt
Karl Rabeder 2014
Das Tao des Glücks
Manuel Schoch 2007
Das große Aura-Praxis-Buch
Richard Webster 2011
Lichtwässer und ihre Heilkräfte
Gudrun Dalla Via 2012
Ich bin da ganz bei Ihnen
Hermann Ehmann 2014
Der Pfad schamanischer Heilung
Alberto Villoldo 2017
Je mehr Löcher, desto weniger Käse
Holger Dambeck 2012
Magie der Heilung
Wolf Wies 2014
Das Zauberbuch für Erwachsene
Michael Engel 2017
Die vierte Dimension
Raul Ibanez 2010
Mit ein bisschen Hilfe von oben
Debra Landwehr Engle 2016
Christliche Prinzipien des politischen Kampfes
Gabriele Kuby 2017
Die verrückte Welt der Paralleluniversen
Tobias Hürter 2011

Weniger ist mehr
Michael Korth 2011
Medizin zum Aufmalen
Petra Neumayer, Roswitha Stark 2012
Die Upanischaden
Eknat Easwaran 2008
Die Zahlenapotheke
Chaseo Rules 2016
Leben nach Maß
Petra Altmann 2009
Das goldene Zeitalter des Christentums
Philip Jenkins 2008
Schariakapitalismus
Sascha Adamek?
Gesund mit Ingwer
Ellen Heidböhmer 2006
Lügen die Medien?
Jens Wernicke 2017
Thich nhat hanh
Celine Chadelat 2017
Gesunde Fette
Dr. Joseph Mercola 2017
Gummizoo macht Kinder froh
Hans-Ulrich Grimm 2017
Albtraum Grenzenlosigkeit
Burkhard Voss 2017
Handlesen
Gertrud I. Hürlimann 2013
Warum Gedanken stärker sind als Medizin
Lissa Rankin 2017
Zellvitalisierung
Dr. med. Rosemarie Unshelm 2017
Ein Lob der Magensäure
Jonathan V. Wright 2016
Die sieben Säulen des Glücks
Abtprimas Notker Wolf 2011

Die Öffnung des 3. Auges
Ulrich Warnke 2017
Jesus, der Zenmeister
Adyashanti 2017
Medizin für die Seele
Sonia Choquette 2010
Becoming Supernatural
Dr. Joe Dispenza 2017
Illusion Tod, DVD
Johann Nepomuk Maier 2017
Jenseits des Greifbaren, DVD
Johann Nepomuk Maier
Vom Ego zur Essenz
Barbara Marx Hubbard 2001
Das Licht auf dem geistigen Pfad
Georg S. Arundale V11
Weckruf der Seele
Paul Ferrini 2016
Geheime Machtstrukturen
Joseph Plummer 2014
Das Rückenheilbuch
Inka Jochum 2020
Deutschland hat Rücken
Roland Liebscher-Bracht 2018
Über die Wahrheit stolpern
Travis Christofferson 2019
Die Urworttheorie, DVD
Dr. Michael König?
Die Diesellüge
Holger Douglas 2018
Energieschnüre
Denise Linn 2019
Gesund mit Wasser und Zeichen
Layena Bassols Rheinfelder 2018
Die entzündete Seele
Edward Bullmore 2018

Der Selbstheilungsnerv
Stanley Rosenberg 2019
Zeitreisen, Heilung für Körper und Geist
Birgit Feliz Carrasco 2016
Die kleine unkorrekte Islambibel
Peter Helmes 2016
Elektromagnetische Felder
Dr. Joseph Mercola
Wir können besser
Clemens G. Arvay 2020
Am Ende ist alles gut
Christina von Dreien 2020
Unerwünschte Wahrheiten
Fritz Vahrenholt, Sebastian Lüning 2020
Der große Impfreport
Neil Z. Miller 2016
Warum sind wir eigentlich noch nicht tot?
Idan Ben-Barak 2017
Leben ohne Pillen
Mirsakarim Norbekov 2020
Parasiten, die heimlichen Krankmacher
Alan E. Baklayan 2018
Die Seele braucht keine Pillen
Dr. med. Kelly Brogdan
Megacrash, Die große Enteignung kommt
Günter Hannich 2018
Freiheit ohne Gott
Werner Münch 2018
Schluss mit euren ewigen Mogelpackungen!
Peter Hahne 2018
Die Regulusbotschaften, Band I bis IV
Bettina Büx 2018
Keto gegen Krebs
Miriam Kalamian 2017
Illegale Kriege
Daniele Ganser 2016

Warum schweigen die Lämmer?
Rainer Mausfeld?
Arthrose heilen mit basischer Ernährung
Rosemarie Muth 2018
Leben wir in einer Illusion?
Lutz Gaudig 2018
Die Ordnung der Zeit
Carlo Rovelli 2018
Nie mehr Parodontose und Karies!
Case Adams 2018
Psi, die Welt ist anders, als sie zu sein scheint
Russell Targ 2013
Verbotene Archäologie
Michael A. Cremo 2006
Heilungsfelder
Larry Dossey 2012
Quantenphilosophie und Spiritualität
Ulrich Warnke 2017
Der Crash ist die Lösung
Matthias Weik 14
12 Rules for Life
Jordan B. Peterson 18
Wohin unsere letzte Reise geht
Beat Imhof 18
Warum die Reichen immer reicher werden
Robert T. Kiyosaki 18
Das große Buch der feinstofflichen Energien
Cyndi Dale 18
Wunderwerk Zirbeldrüse
Stefan Limmer 18
Die Psychologie der Anziehungskraft
Vanessa Van Edwards 18
Entdecke deinen Geburtsengel
Chamuel Schauffert 18
Besser hören – leichter leben
Anton Stucki 18

Tore zum kosmischen Bewusstsein
Anthony Peake 17
Weltverschwörung
Thomas A. Anderson 16
Mensch: Gemacht
Gregg Braden 18
Die Wiederentdeckung der Spiritualität
Rupert Sheldrake 17
Der Diktatorpapst
Marcantonio Colonna 18
Multiple Sklerose und (sehr viel) Vitamin D
Ana Claudia Domene 18
Wie der Rücken die Seele und die Seele den Rücken heilt
Kurt Mosetter 15
Auracoaching
Bahar Yilmaz 13
Zaubertrank, liposomal verkapseltes Vitamin C
Dr. med. Eberhard J. Wormer 18
Der Ruf der geistigen Welt
Bahar Yilmaz 14
Bruno Gröning, Das geheimnisvolle Leben ...
Mara Macri 15
DNA-Aktivierung durch die kosmische Familie
Eva Marquez 16
Welten im Zusammenstoß
Dr. Immanuel Velikovsky
Der Weg des Meisters
Christopher Po Minar 18
Das große Buch der Energieheilung
Kalashatra Govinda, Fei Long 18
Die implizite Ordnung
David Bohm 18
Die Kraft der Acht
Lynne McTaggart 17
Heilung ohne Medizin
Albert Amao 15

Gestorben ist noch lange nicht tot
Penny McLean 18
Bridging Two Realms
John Holland 18
Das große Buch der Akashachronik
Daniel Meurois 18
Covid-19: Der große Umbruch
Klaus Schwab 20
Weltsystem Crash
Max Otte 19
Die Krise hält sich nicht an Regeln
Max Otte 21
Die Aminorevolution
Dr. med. Ulrich Strunz 21
Der Gottesbeweis
Deepak Chopra 2014
Zieht euch warm an, es wird heiß
Sven Plöger 2020
Keto-Cycling
Bruce Fife 2019
Keto-Fasten
Dr. Joseph Mercola 2019
Ketogene Ernährung für Einsteiger
Jimmy Moore 2016
77 Tipps für ein gesundes Gehirn
Dr. med. Ulrich Strunz 2020
Wir erleben mehr, als wir begreifen
Hans-Peter Dürr
Der 4-Stunden-Körper
Timothy Ferriss
Diät-Revolution
Dr. Robert Atkins 2018/1972
Heile deine Schilddrüse
Anthony William 2018
Entfalte deine Lebensenergie
Rajshree Patel 2019

Geheimnisse von Raum und Zeit
Walter Bloch 2020
Power fürs Gehirn
Felix Mayer 2018
Mit Geld zur Weltherrschaft
Thorsten Polleit 2020
Söhne und Weltmacht
Gunnar Heinsohn 2019
China am Ziel
Christoph Leitl 2020
Die Smartphone-Epidemie
Manfred Spitzer 2018
3 – 6 – 5 Der Atem-Code
David O'Hare
Kundalini Yoga als Seelenreise
Satya Singh 2019
Christina, Band 3: Bewusstsein schafft Frieden
Christina von Dreien 2019
Heile deine Leber
Anthony William 2019
Die Allergiebibel
Dr. Earl Mindell, Dr. Pamela Wartian Smith 2018
Vergiss deine Brille
Leo Angart 2018
Kinder brauchen keine Brille
Leo Angart 2020
Wieder lesen ohne Brille
Leo Angart 2019
Eine kurze Geschichte von jedem ...
Adam Rutherford
Die bürgerliche Revolution
Markus Krall 2020
Superheilmittel Vitamin C
Thomas E. Levy 2017
Neues aus Absurdistan
Luc Bürgin 2020

Das Alter als Geschenk
Ruediger Dahlke 2018
Geo-Imperialismus
Wolfgang Effenberger 2016
Das Enneagramm: Die 9 Gesichter der Seele
Richard Rohr 2019
Ohne Worte: Was andere über dich denken
Thorsten Havener 2014
Warum ist $E = mc^2$?
Brian Cox, Jeff Forshaw 2018
Das kosmische Hologramm
Jude Currivan 2020
Tore ins unendliche Bewusstsein
Dr. med. Eben Alexander 2017
Junge Seelen – alte Seelen
Varda Hasselmann, Frank Schmolke 2020
Herr bleibe bei uns
Robert Kardinal Sarah 2019
Das Wörterbuch der Lügenpresse
Thor Kunkel 2020
Verzockte Freiheit
Markus Krall 2014
Die Denkfabriken
F. William Engdahl 2015
Aus toten Böden wird fruchtbare Erde
Gabe Brown 2020
Sicherheitsrisiko Islam
Stefan Schubert 2019
Gesundheit in unseren Händen – mit Mudras zu mehr Lebenskraft
Kim da Silva 2019
Innere Heilung
Alex Loyd 2019
Offiziell geleugnet!
Steven M. Greer
Die Mission der Seele
Robert Schwartz 2019

Was tun?
David Engels 2020
Der Koran auf dem Prüfstand
Eberhard Kleina 2019
Fremdenergien
Claus Walter 2019
Feldzug gegen die Nation
Viktor Timtschenko 2019
Das Ende des Alterns
Prof. Dr. David A. Sinclair 2019
Das kleine Handbuch des Stoizismus
Jonas Salzgeber 2020
Die Kräuter in meinem Garten
Siegrid Hirsch 2020
Mythos Klimakatastrophe, DVD
Marco Pino
Freiheit oder Untergang
Markus Krall 2021
Die Welt-Kraft in dir
Roger D. Nelson, Georg Kindel 2021
Naturwissenschaft und Religion
Ken Wilber 1998
Alles Leben ist eins (Die Begegnung von Quantenphysik und Mystik)
Renee Weber 1986
Was uns krank macht, was uns heilt
Christian Schubert 2021, 7. Auflage
Great Reset
Dr. C. E. Nyder Mai 2021
Das Corona-Dossier
Flo Osrainik 2021, 2. Auflage
Abnehmen am Bauch
Sarah Schocke 2021, 3. Auflage
Folge der Kraft des Samurai
Lori Tsugawa Whaley 2021
Freiheit in Gefahr

Hans-Jürgen Papier 2021
Corona-Impfungen aus spiritueller Sicht
Thomas Mayer 2021
Junge globale Führerin – Annalena Baerbock
Michael Grandt
Vater Eiche – Mutter Linde
Alfred Zenz 2019
Was will Putin?
Stephan Berndt 2015
Praxisbuch CDL (Chlordioxid)
Brigitte Hamann 2021
Die Welt mit anderen Augen sehen
Markholf H. Niemz 2020
Chronik einer angekündigten Krise
Paul Schreyer 2020
Der Griff in die Kasse
Hans Herbert von Arnim 2020
Der Corona-Schock
Hans-Werner Sinn 2020
Die Revolution ist fällig
Albrecht Müller 2020
Würde – Was uns stark macht
Gerald Hüther 2018
Qigong
Kenneth Cohen 2020
Megamanipulation
Ulrich Mies 2020
Warum wir mehr als einmal auf Erden leben
Beat Imhof 2020
Der größte Crash aller Zeiten
Marc Friedrich, Matthias Weik 2019
Der Garten der Druiden
Dr. Claudia Urbanovsky 2020
Change!: Warum wir eine radikale Wende brauchen
Graeme Maxton 2018
Der große Neustart

Wellem Middelkoop 2015
Wir sind das Klima
Jonathan Safran Foer 2019
Der Tag, an dem wir aufhören zu shoppen
J. B. MacKinnon 2021
Endspiel des Kapitalismus
Norbert Häring 2021
Sklavenplanet Erde – Es ist Zeit, aufzuwachen!
Gabriele Schuster-Haslinger 2019
Evolution 2021
Dieter Broers & Freunde 2nd expanded edition
Die wundersame Geldvermehrung
Hans-Werner Sinn 2021
Ich hatte nicht immer, was ich wollte, aber alles, was ich brauchte:
Erkenntnisse aus meinem Leben als buddhistischer Mönch
Björn Natthiko Lindeblad 2020
Jenseits von Materie
Prof. Dr. Oliver S. Lazar 2021, 3rd edition
Naturgeister – Wahre Begegnungen mit Elfen und Zwergen
Annekatrin Puhle, Mary Tulloch 2016, 3rd edition
Strommangelwirtschaft
Henrik Paulitz 2020
Der Weg beginnt unter deinen Füßen
Jeff Shore 2018
Der Welt-Geist: Wie wir alle miteinander verbunden sind
Roger D. Nelson 2018
Verjüngung ist möglich
Nina Ruge, Dr. Dr. med. Dominik Duscher 2021
Klimadämmerung
Frank Hennig 2021, 3rd edition
Wenn Beteigeuze explodiert
Stephan Bernt 2021
Die Urquelle der Glückseligkeit
Ulrich Warnke 2021
5G – Die geheime Gefahr
Dr. med. Joachim Mutter 2021

BOOK FIVE

THE 6TH KONDRATIEV

Where did all these books come from? 20 pages with 15 titles, equals 300, mainly from 2009, 3000 books in my private library. All my questions have been answered. I became a MEDICAL SPECIALIST FOR "HUMOR", as far as I know, the only one in the world. That would be the 34th specialty (there are clinical and theoretical ones). These authors are the REGIMENT 3000! Everything that holds the world together at its core is described. Anyone can provide dietary counseling and talk therapy without a license to practice. The 1st Kondratiev was the invention of the steam engine.

These are waves that decisively move society forward.

The theme of the 6th Kondratiev is knowledge, health, and the environment. Far beyond school-level knowledge and health in all areas. And so the solution to all our problems has been named. Graeme Maxton's "Change! Warum wir eine radikale Wende brauchen".

2018
EARTH RESOURCE DAY LIES IN THE MIDDLE OF SUMMER.

The FOURIER PRINCIPLE (pantry monitoring) applies. One child figured it out: "In 20 years, the earth won't be here anymore!" Calculation of the most powerful computers: everything will collapse in 2050! Humanity will become extinct in a short time, just like the dinosaurs! Greed for profit and striving for material wealth (prosperity) prevail. India and China: "First we want prosperity like Europe, then we will get to the environment, let's say sometime around 2060!" The second problem: I saw a documentary about the U.S. at 2°C (3.6°F) of global warming. All TIPPING POINTS had been reached, the world population was wiped out like the dinosaurs! The 2-degree Celsius limit is lethal, and that also applies to the rest of the world's population! Paris 2015: INCREASE BY 1.5° CELSIUS STILL MANAGEABLE!!! So far, we've had an increase in temperature by roughly 1.1°C worldwide. A. Guterres (UN) is desperate: +3 degrees by 2050 despite all measures!! This means that the final climate catastrophe will come several years earlier. Problem: DEFORESTATION OF THE RAINFOREST IN BRAZIL. I watched a documentary about the over-exploitation of the rainforest. The forest has a VALUE of 1 TRILLION DOLLARS PER DAY!!! It tips the scales for the world climate (arid, humid). President Bolsonaro: soy for China, beef, tropical timber. He wants the mineral resources and thereby create prosperity for all. 133 leaders of the indigenous people have already been killed by the timber mafia.

DEFORESTATION CONTINUES – 2030 IS THE END – 16 TIPPING POINTS!! Prof. Harald Lesch: "The end for humanity!" Then you will realize the deep shit you're sitting in, worldwide, when nobody can do anything anymore – humanity's demise. Dr. Eckart von Hirschhausen: "Then it's game over!"

Spiritual Knowledge: "17th" UNIVERSAL LAW. MATHEMATICS OF GOD: We can watch him at work. 8-4, BOLZO, offers him 100 billion euros for 10 years of rainforest. Stops the purchase of tropical timber, beef, soy for pigs! KARMA AND REINCARNATION = spiritual basic law. Death star of billions of souls – no reincarnation possible anymore! Human development from animal to material life, SOCIETY FORMATIONS; slaves, aristocracy, capitalists. The Kondratiev effects a leap to the next level. PARADIGM SHIFT to the PRIMACY OF THE SPIRIT!!! Away from material wealth to social, mental, psychological … F-LEAP: FORTE, EVOLUTIONARY JUMP!!! Every single person becomes a global thinker, accepting God at the helm. ECONOMY: MAJOR TRANSFORMATION, sustainable (everything can be recycled), ecological, social, fair. It has to start now, time until 2030! PRIMACY OF SPIRIT rises ABOVE the basic law of capitalism: STRIVE FOR MAXIMUM PROFIT!!! The new motto is: Public interest comes before self-interest. Monopoly capitalism in this form has had its day: it is stinking, rotting, parasitic, and moribund! It was a policy mistake of the last decades: Capital was taxed much less than labor.

Put a stop to shareholders on the stock exchange: financial transaction tax! Large corporations have paid absolutely no taxes at all for decades. VALUE ADDING LAW – Labor yields more value than it costs – gratuitous appropriation by the capitalist (investments). The customer comes first. Supply and demand are what matters. And yet politicians follow the lobbyists ... There are now 3,000 billionaires worldwide (800 more since the coronavirus). In the Roman Empire, a Jubilee year was proclaimed every 50 years: Debts were canceled, slaves were set free. Today, a few in the background have the say over 80 trillion dollars!!! It's not about drawing a demonizing stereotype here ... This amount of money is needed for environmental technology and conversion/reconstruction. Currently, value is created using debt. Money is printed and bank deposits are stored electronically. This bubble will lead to a global financial crash (coordinated?). GLOBAL UPHEAVAL OF THE FINANCIAL SYSTEM is imminent.

Sustainable agriculture is needed: Less meat and dairy products – meat will soon be produced in vitro! The current fertilization method produces dead soil. The future: permaculture! PLANET-HEALTH-DIET, eat what the planet produces in the long term. FREE ENERGY TECHNOLOGY (FET) is the GAME CHANGER!!! After the initial investment, electricity is very cheap – EL DORADO!!! All world religions will be united under one umbrella. TIME FOR F-LEAP AT ONCE, EVERY SINGLE PERSON NOW. Rap BOLZO's knuckles!

We want a social market economy without blatant inequality in wealth. In principle, the F-leap should also work without FET. "I'm a lateral thinker and I'm not going to go along with this whole thing." "Read it again, even special-needs students understand, or are you pro-Death Star? We'll sear the 84 into your aura and onto your forehead!" "Get on board, we're way past the 11th hour!" This is the PLANET PLAN, the "BLUE MARBLE PROJECT."

Philosopher Hegel: Elevating to the level of "PRIMACY OF THE SPIRIT", save everything that can be used. In summary: Every single person consciously performs the F-jump! We've got 8 years of hard work ahead of us, then the road to El Dorado begins! How much does the Blue Marble project cost? The hearts and minds of 8 billion people! For debt relief for poor countries, against exploitation. Drawing from my Kondratiev library, I would like to highlight the following book: Dr. Norbert Häring's "Endspiel des Kapitalismus" (Capitalism's Endgame – How the Corporations Took Power and How We're Taking It Back". 2021: end of factory farming, all the feed comes from abroad! "BLUE MARBLE": THE PEOPLE HAVE TO WANT IT. The Germans live as if we had 3 Earths, worldwide 1.75 Earths. EARTH for all – eliminate extreme inequality! Nearly 85 people own as much as half of all humanity. Lentil soup and flatbread ensure basic nutrition. EQUAL RIGHTS FOR WOMEN!!! It is a Herculean task to guide the Spirit of the Lord into all minds. This is the strategy and tactics of the Plan for the Planet! Brisant TV: Mojib Latif: CO_2 – Germany down 40%, world up 60% ... $380 billion annually for coal subsidies worldwide!!! USA – 6,000 patents "dangerous to the state", and why is that? "Fossil." In sum: move away from the "Death Star" – Bolzo! Onward to "El Dorado!" F-leap FET is the game changer.

From material egotism to spiritual-globally thinking Homo Sapiens.

RELIGION

In the natural sciences, experiments are considered demonstrative proof.

Imagine the following experiment: A person is hypnotized and given the following task: Leave your body, go into the next room and see what's inside (painter, judoka, violinist). Return to your body and report back once you wake up! This is exactly how it works all over the world – the test person (subject) had fulfilled their task! You can also experience what are called regressions in hypnosis! You go back in time to your birth and then to the previous life and beyond! This means that every human being has an ethereal core (soul), which stores everything and reaches the "beyond" after death! This "place" is now better explored than the deep sea. Germany's most famous death researcher, Bernard Jakoby, has written 5 books about near-death experiences and the passage to "heaven". We also know that there is no sex in the beyond (a soul is sexless) and there is no food. Islamic martyrs are promised about 72 houris (virgins) after crossing over. By all means, if that's what they believe in. Dr. Eben Alexander and Don Piper were clinically dead, had looked at everything "over there" and returned to their bodies. The most prominent example of rebirth is the Dalai Lama, whose name means "Ocean of Knowledge!" His soul has already entered a human body 13 times. During his lifetime, he can predict approximately where and when he will be reborn and can be found. He is no longer the political leader of the Tibetans because they now have a democratic parliament (government in exile). Furthermore, he leaves it up to his peers to decide whether he should return to Earth again as the Dalai Lama. He also initiated a 17-year study of Tibetan Buddhism for women. We've got the mathematics of God: He shows Himself especially in "dynamic" numbers (17, 34, 51, 84, also 48, 96, 69). But the Lord is at least one dimension higher, because He works everywhere at the same time (Holy

Spirit) and knows the thoughts of the people. Everyone is connected to him – he's got everyone on his radar! We just don't have a sensory organ for this immense intelligence! Or do you truly believe that he does not know whether a conceived child will be aborted or not, and therefore lets the soul incarnate or not? Apart from that, everything we have explored so far in the world only amounts to 4% of the universe – everything else is dark matter/energy!

Freedom of faith applies on Earth! If you believe that "A cow shitting on my doorstep is good luck!", then go ahead. 300 million women have had their clitorises circumcised (equivalent to cutting the glans off a man's penis), believing they are now "grown up!" 8-4, but knowledge goes beyond that, 6th Kondratiev.

Islam – a great religion / Allahu Akbar – God is the greatest / was the bridge from the Orient to the Occident / men can have up to 4 wives, who do not need to work, do not have to go to school, can take care of the children / Kismet = faith in fate / convert and prophet's blasphemy: death penalty / bow towards Mecca 5 times daily / woman: eye contact with men = invitation to have sex / swimming burka, women are not allowed to drive a car / jihad / fatwah / world caliphate, Koran – archangel Gabriel – Mohammed, Koran schools in Pakistan (financed by Iran), free room and board, 6,000 Afghans / Sharia: A woman was whipped, she had talked to a man on the phone / cheating wife – stoning, become married as a virgin, long veil / no alcohol, headscarf / no pork / Shiites – Sunnis. All of this may be believed and these traditions lived by!

What is Islam missing? A Mahdi (expected savior of the Mohammedans)! And who could we pick for this? Jesus, the son of God (Allah) is the only one who comes to mind!!!

And Jesus is responsible for the whole world anyway.

"Death to the infidels!" is now dropped because there are no more non-believers in the world! (Primacy of the Spirit.) Jesus is already omnipresent and not the devil, as the Bible claims. There is no figure with such great, negative power! Evil comes forth through corrupt people. A return of the Messiah with a resurrection of the dead is unlikely! "He who believes in Me, as the Scripture has said, will have streams of living water flow from deep within him!" (Holy Spirit – God's working power). I recommend everyone read at least the New Testament of the Bible! In Asian religions, the idea of a cyclical world predominates: Buddhism (to be enlightened), Hinduism (outdated caste system), nevertheless also their God "Yahweh" stands over everything, faith – knowledge!

A word about communists and materialists: Death is a taboo topic for them because they think: "Now life is over and so is everything else!" In China, civil servants used to have to memorize the writings of Confucius – the three-day exam was taken naked!!! Now you've got a surveillance state with facial recognition and cell phone tracking. "A bird will always prefer a simple twig over a golden cage!" Jesus knows the thoughts of every Chinese, you can never reproduce "Chi-Chi." Let Jesus be your servant, he will kiss your feet! The other day God woke me up at night and said to me, "Turn on the radio!" A song by Heinz-Rudolf Kunze: "It's time for a huge awakening and a silver lining will give us hope!"

FREE ENERGY TECHNOLOGY (FET)

Please read the first two pages of the literature list again! My 1st book on this topic: Andreas von Retýi, "Energie ohne Ende" (Energy without End), 2013 Then Claus W. Turtur, 2014, "Freie Energie für alle Menschen, Raumenergiemotor: Nachweis und Bauanleitung" (Free Energy for Everyone, Free spatial energy engine: proof and construction manual) – I was thrilled!!! Free energy exists. And we can harness it. This is the proof! Energy that is inexhaustible and available everywhere, costs nothing, generates electricity, does not pollute the environment and health. Can such a thing exist? School-level science says, "No!" As do energy companies and the establishment. By contrast, Claus W. Turtur claims: Inexhaustible energy, which offers all these advantages, does exist. And we can harness it. This is because free energy allows us to build generators that solve humanity's supply problems once and for all. So far, we have been burning tons of coal and gasoline to release the energy of a single megawatt hour. At the same time, one liter of pure space contains 27,811,799 billion megawatt-hours. A one-off investment of 2,000 euros in this source – and your electricity and heating costs, as well as your gasoline bill would be taken care of for the next 20 to 30 years! Prof. Turtur's favorite book: "Urkraft aus dem Universum und Nikola Teslas Pierce Arrow 8", Adolf und Inge Schneider, Klaus Jebens, January 2022, Jupiter-Verlag.

The greatest moment in the life of co-author Klaus Jebens, who died in 2014, was when in 2001 he discovered in his father Heinrich's old files a strictly confidential memo dated December 9, 1930. It concerned his ride in Nikola Tesla's legendary Pierce Arrow 8 using a free energy drive. Jebens felt it was time to publish this note because of the escalating energy crisis. That was the start of his engagement with free energy. He founded an institute and has invested his fortune in the construction of a free energy device. Many have followed in his footsteps. In 2017, Adolf Schneider wrote a leaflet about the Arrow 8 on behalf of the German Association for Space Energy. In the book's chapter "Real Free Energy Systems and Prospects" there are reports about fully developed devices.

A water engine ...to build yourself for motorcycles and cars! Adolf and Inge Schneider, Jose Vaesken Guillen, 2018 I have taken the following passages from the book: Water as a new source of energy according to Prof. P. Kanarev. Prof. Phillip M. Kanarev's lecture at the 2001 Jupiter Publishing House Hydrogen Congress in Weinfelden was one of the highlights of this event. At that time, Prof. Kanarev already used his theoretical model and practical laboratory experiments in the video to show that electrolysis of water is possible. It requires only about 1/10 of the energy input that is common in traditional electrolysis. He was able to prove that the energy required for hydrogen production is 10 to 15 times lower with the newly developed plasma-electrolytic generator. In other words, Kanarev's reactors have an efficiency of 1,000 to 1,500%. Even though Prof. Kanarev was able to prove the function of his 3 kW and 6 kW plasma reactor in experiments, his work is not scientifically recognized to this day because there is no underlying theory for it. This will continue until the world urgently needs new energy sources and recognizes them. Ecologically pure energy sources will become available to humanity in the near future.

Nicholas Moller's atomic hydrogen generator MAHG ... He emphasized that solutions should not be expected from the establishment, however, but from idealists who care about the state of the planet. If you look at the conventional way of producing hydrogen (e.g., for fuel cell cars), it becomes evident that 4 times the amount of energy has to be used compared to the output. With this technology, it would take another 100 nuclear power plants to supply the energy to produce hydrogen – a proportion that is nonsensical. Furthermore, if hydrogen is produced from natural gas and burned in a fuel cell, it depletes oxygen from the atmosphere. There are solutions, such as the 80% efficient splitting method or the cold fusion method by the Japanese scientist Mizuno, which can produce 8 times more hydrogen than traditional electrolysis methods.

The core of the invention refers to the partial electrolysis of water through electrical energy with the formation of atomic hydrogen at high temperatures, which, however, quickly recombines into the familiar hydrogen molecule. This results in a significant release of heat, which can be used in principle to provide the energy for electrolysis. Thus an autonomous cycle could be realized. Inventor Nicholas Moller attributed the effects of harnessing hydrogen-bonding energy to the use of pulsed direct currents.

In this context, MAHG researchers sometimes also spoke of cold fusion of the present hydrogen atoms to form the H2 hydrogen molecule. Both Prof. Kanarev and Irving Langmuir, like Nicholas Moller, believe that the invention could achieve a COP of 2001. This successful course could not be continued, however, and the UN failed to work with them.

Nanopulse electrolysis from India – 31 times more effective in gas recovery:
Every electrolytic cell will eventually reach the maximum value of gas that the cell can produce as the current is increased. This max. value of the gas volume, which the scientists could generate in their series of experiments, was 0.58 ml/s. 18 watts were needed with direct current to produce this amount of gas. When using their pulse circuit, on the other hand, it was only 0.57 watts. That corresponds to an energy saving of 96.8% compared to conventional electrolysis with direct current. This invention only became publicly known in 2018. At the time, the authors received information from several sources. The word was that the scientists had succeeded experimentally in demonstrating that water could be broken down into its gaseous components much more effectively with nanopulse electrolysis than with conventional, direct-current electrolysis. This then begged the question: will cars even need energy storage in the future? If we are to believe the Indian researchers, then no! It is possible that vacuum energy from space-time is converted into real energy. In conclusion: nanopulse electrolysis is 31.58 times more effective than direct current electrolysis. This system only produces as much gas as is needed to power a vehicle. Such a car essentially runs on water!

What is Aqua Flex?
It is a mixture of alcohol and water, which can have different blending levels, depending on the type of engine and combustion

chamber. The maximum water content is 80%. The remaining 20% is alcohol. With this mixture, the engine functions the same as with a pure gasoline operation and achieves the same performance values. For example, with an engine with eight valves and a fuel mixture of 30% alcohol and 70% water, the engine runs as usual without any temperature or starting problems (José Vaesken Guillen).

Auf dem Weg in das Raumenergiezeitalter (On the Path to the Free Energy Age), Adolf and Inge Schneider, 2020.

I took the following passages from this book: With his lectures and the wonderful definitive work "Raumenergie- Technik – weltweit der vorteilhafteste Weg zur Nachhaltigkeit der Energieversorgung," Prof. (em.) Dr. Dr. h.c. Josef Gruber made a decisive contribution to the free energy movement. Among other things, he talks about Daimler-Chrysler's A-Class car with Ballard's methanol-powered fuel cell, called NECAR 5, which at the time had made a record trip from San Francisco to Washington D.C. (3,262 miles). He also mentioned Prof. Yull Brown's highly efficient electrolysis cell (Brown's Gas), in which water was broken down into a mixture of hydrogen and oxygen using electricity from a wall socket. Quote: "In my opinion, it must be possible to soon run electric cars such as NECAR on hydrogen as a fuel, produced on-demand in the electric car using Yull Brown's method. That would be a 'quantum leap' toward sustainability, at least in the transportation sector." The question arises as to how Europe is set up in the field of free energy technology, and all this in a Europe "where scientists, politicians and businesspeople are primarily concerned with maintaining power rather than finding real solutions."

He had seen a demo unit on July 2nd, 1993 at a highway service station in Kassel, which may not have worked autonomously, but in a way that should not have been possible according to the physical theorems. Following this experience, he decided to dedicate himself to free energy technology, because he recognized in it not only "the biggest technical revolution in technology", but also t h e environmental solution par excellence.

According to him, this is less a technical challenge than a political one. From Tom Bearden's Motionless Electromagnetic Generator MEG to the Patterson Cell to the Casimir Effect, many effects and devices would show that free energy exists and that it can be harnessed.

Quote: "Today, the question is no longer whether free energy can be used, but whether the public is ready for it." He explains that politics and business are great preventers of such technologies. He gathered the information about free energy devices for his book at international conferences, including those in the U.S., Russia, and in Europe. After the book was published, he sent 300 copies on his own account to ministers, economists, and politicians in German-speaking European regions.

At least the office of German Chancellor Angela Merkel called him to express their thanks, but hardly anyone else responded. The speaker stated that "At least no one can say they didn't know!" With free energy, decentralized energy supply is possible, overhead power lines and transformer stations could be dismantled. So the aim is for science to recognize free energy as a primary power source.

Accordingly, the indifferent public includes anyone who does nothing. He therefore addressed the participants with a call to action at the end: "Join in, help build the free energy age!"

The Quantum Energy Generator QEG:
In 2014, an open-source project from the U.S., the Quantum Energy Generator (QEG), was launched by Hope Moore, who later became known as "Hope Girl," and her stepfather James Robitaille. They founded the group "Fix the World" for this purpose. It was a self-running energy machine that could be replicated by anyone. She said she wanted to bring "hope to the world" with the QEG. She was an ordinary person, trained as a financial analyst, but motivated to contribute to the reorganization and redistribution of resources in the world. The topic of energy seemed extremely important to her in this regard.

News about the existence of such an energy machine dropped like a bomb: a free-energy project that anyone could replicate! A peace project that should bring people together, a resonance project. "...It became clear to me that this is my task on Earth, what I was born to do."

The QEG is an adaptation of an electric generator-dynamo design patented by Nikola Tesla on October 2, 1888. In fact, the first QEG prototypes were built by Timothy Thrapp as early as 2008. He demonstrated a self-running motor-generator in March 2009. The design was intended for a 40-kW motor, but it was demonstrated with a load of 15 kW. It's worth noting that Timothy Thrapp built the QEG based on patents by Nikola Tesla and John W. Ecklin, which were always open-source. Nonetheless, Timothy Thrapp proved that the QEG itself works. That is why the authors felt it was important to publish the information about the QEG, the plans and further developments in their book "The Quantum Energy Generator". The field is highly interesting for researchers, users, and experimenters and is far from being fully explored ...

Neutrino voltaics – energy from the cosmos:
Holger Thorsten Schubart, CEO of the Neutrino Energy Group, you could also call him "Mister Neutrino"! The authors met with him on June 26, 2015. At that time, he showed them a short video on his phone, featuring a polymer film on an aluminum layer that was capable of generating electricity without exposure to light. He was convinced that neutrinos were "the energy of the future". 380,000 years after the creation of the universe, as astrophysicists have calculated, there were still 15% photons, i.e. light particles, and 10% neutrinos in the cosmos. These are the particles of the so-called weak interaction. In other words, we can say that a neutrino weighs 500,000 times less than an electron. It should be noted that neutrinos are not "captured" in any way nor is their mass transformed into energy according to Einstein's formula. Rather, it is a matter of transferring kinetic energy of individual neutrinos to the atoms in the very

dense graphene layers via resonance coupling. In this process, the tightly packed fabric structures of the graphene are stimulated to vibrate vertically. This in turn generates horizontal movements in the silicon layer. The electrical current is then decoupled via electrical contacts on opposite edges. This technology is called neutrino voltaics. Experience has shown that enough films to produce a micro power plant with a capacity of 4.5 to 5.5 kW could fit into a "pilot's case."

Since neutrino energy is constantly available everywhere, such a small power plant continuously produces electricity. This could, for example, happen in a moving electric car. Consequently, only a small battery would be needed in the car for peak power demands, such as during extreme situations like uphill driving and acceleration. Charging stations for electric cars would become obsolete.

With neutrino technology, electric cars would be significantly cheaper, as expensive batteries can be replaced with smaller, more affordable versions.

The range of electric cars would dramatically increase at the same time, since they would largely generate their energy needs. This could be achieved by coating the entire surface of an electric car so that neutrinos, through resonance processes, induce electrons to produce electricity.

The prospects for the use of this immense energy source for electricity generation are promising and as extensive as the energy itself. After the book "Das ewige Licht – der Beginn eines neuen Zeitalters" (The Eternal Light – the Dawning of a New Age) by Prof. Günther Krause about neutrino technology was also published in late August 2020, Holger Thorsten Schubart enthusiastically informed the authors: "It's happening!"

So we will stay tuned to these exciting developments ...

The Letsini Generator:
What made Letsini's design unique was that the rotor carried electromagnets that, when passing by a corresponding electromagnet

on the stator at a speed of 1,500 rpm, induced an alternating current of 50 Hz. The system was meant to be started manually and then would carry on autonomously after the first 5 revolutions. The rotor, which was to be driven by an electric motor, acted via a transmission belt on an alternator, which was to supply the energy for the motor drive and for the pulsed energizing of the rotor's electromagnets. Battery buffered charging is not required, according to the inventor. According to the data sheet, the system consumed 100 watts but could deliver about 1.5 kW at the output.

The inventor informed the authors that he had a working prototype in Cameroon. He was looking for investors interested in global patenting and acquiring production licenses.

Regarding the Letsini device, a team of experts was formed in August 2020 with the aim of definitively enabling this autonomous 3 kW system to operate autonomously. The prospects look good!

Bulltechnik – autonomous power generation with Jupiter generator:

Rolf Kranen, the inventor of Bulltechnik and the owner of the Fixtron company, is an exceptional figure in the field of new energy technologies and free energy, not just from a technical standpoint. Rolf Kranen says his biggest concern is building and providing alternatives for nuclear power plants and other technologies that extract raw materials from the earth. He is dedicating his life to this goal. His presentation at the Energy Fair in Essen was a great success and very well received by the audience. The regional TV station broadcast an interview with Rolf Kranen, during which he said, among other things, "It's a new way of generating energy. We are creating a new energy process in a centrifuge – a physical phenomenon. We intend to further refine it in our Bulltechnik research. The function can be demonstrated at our testing facility. This phenomenon induces a flow process that produces endless energy at a constant speed. The phenomenon is that the process inside the system continues without slowing down the system.

It is possible to release 65 kW with a centrifuge. These systems can produce endless electricity for decades. The jets need to be replaced every 10 or 20 years, similar to how spark plugs need to be replaced in a car. Otherwise, such systems are maintenance-free.

These centrifuges can also generate electricity underground. The units are cylindrical rotors running at 180 rpm. Depending on the height, they only need 50 to 80 W to maintain the revolution speed. A cold weather system of cold gases is formed at the top and a fluid system of liquefied gas is formed at the bottom. This way, heat always flows toward the cold. Between these layers are plates, called Seebeck or thermoelectric generators. As heat flows through them, electrical energy is released. For every layer between cold and hot, we can produce electricity in a future plant on 8 by 8 feet with 1,200 Peltier elements. The heat flow generated in the plant is directly converted into a flow of energy. The plus cable is on the top, the minus cable on the bottom. Even while the process is working inside and continuously releases energy, the rotary motion does not slow down.

Responding to a TV journalist on when the first systems will go online, Rolf Kranen replied, "The processes are already working in our prototypes. All we have to do now is find an exact match in the systems so that we can get optimum current values at the optimum unit size. Our planning target is to have the first series-produced units ready by early 2022. At the same time, we are trying to buy up industrial plants in various countries with our sales partners, so that regional industrial plants can mass-produce the devices in each country. This allows us to quickly and effectively provide electricity without CO_2 and radioactive pollutants. That's our goal!"

"Yes, the second law of thermodynamics needs to be expanded. While it does apply in the stationary system, it is different for the rotating system. A gyro weighs 3.5 oz when it is idle, for example. When it is spinning at 5,000 rpm, it still weighs 3.5 oz on the outside, but 1.1 tons in certain places on the inside."

"Anyway, I don't think fusion reactors are our future – I generate merely 80 degrees at 25 bar."

According to Prof. Josef Gruber's assessment, the introduction of free energy technologies as a whole will lead to "a lasting economic and environmental miracle."
Plenty of reason to celebrate!
End of the quote.

That was just the tip of the iceberg. There are many more possibilities!!!
Once you make the F-leap, you will have power without end!!! Of course, FET must not fall into the wrong hands (profiteering). 6,000 patents are blocked by "fossil opponents" in the U.S. There are also poor losers (plutocratic neo-feudalism).
Which came first, the chicken or the egg?

Energy sources beyond school knowledge are denied to the population. The latest systems purge CO_2 from the air. One ton of CO_2 = 60 euros, later up to 20 euros (filtering out). With enough H2 and electricity, syngas for gas heating and e-fuels are also possible. (In Germany, there are 48.7 million internal combustion engines = backbone of the economy.) Coal-fired power generation annually worldwide: 380 billion euros in subsidies (in addition there would be CO_2 tax), most expensive and most detrimental energy! FET must be developed in a decentralized manner (honeycomb method). Grid operators demand 5% return on investment (the end for "Südlink Thüringen"). Wind turbines provide only 10% domestically on 100 days a year. Minister Altmeier wanted to board up and wire up Germany for 2 trillion euros. Germany only contributes 2% of global CO_2 but serves as a role model for the entire world. Nuclear fusion is a 23-billion-euro money pit (no money for Turtur, etc.!). "E-cars: 17 tons of CO_2 during production" – unacceptable (transformation). Nuclear power plants = dinosaur technology (legacy costs in the billions).
FET – effective on a mass scale! Fossil – over, over, over, the game is over!

Germany is the world champion!

Soccer World Cup 1954, Bern, from now on we have "Fritz Walter weather"! Palm oil is 4 times more harmful to the climate than conventional fuel. Coal company wants to sue a Benelux country for one trillion euros – we'll sue them for the value of the Earth (8-4)! The UN plan includes 17 points (do not count on F-leap)! António Guterres, UN General Secretary: "Blue Marble Project!" followed by a battle cry! May it curdle the blood of the Bolsojanos! Primacy of the spirit!

CORONAVIRUS

From January 20, 2017, to January 20, 2021, Trump was the 45th President of the USA. Famous Spanish freedom fighter El Cid (the Lord). El Merk – Germany's El Trump or Hillary Clinton – Scylla or Charybdis? The U.S. chose both! El Trump ordered a program from Cambridge Analytics. For example, gun owners received an email: "Clinton opposes private weapons!" Putin intercepted Clinton's email traffic – certain parts kept showing up online. The policy of "America first" means America will die first (!). El Trump – a cunning real estate speculator! He told 20,000 lies throughout his tenure! Climate deniers ("someone made it up!"), and thus blasphemers! That makes El Trump satanic thoughts incarnate – Death Star!! USA: 20 tons of CO_2 per person per year!!

Wuhan – coronavirus: a small animals market or a laboratory? The leak: lab accident with bats (American money and researchers). In El Trump's time, the national debt increased by $2 trillion! Conservative Republicans: Keep everything the way it is. Construction of a wall along the Mexican border. Bolsonaros – Rainforest

Logger of Brazil – Axis of (D)evil – El Trump. He did not lead during the pandemic – crucial loss of votes!!!

Joe Biden not perfect – 7 million more voters / electors, nevertheless. The mail-in ballots were decisive and turned the tide! (From now on, I don't want to see anyone vote for the Alternative for the Dumb). Trump (no more safe abortions) has "circumcised" childbearing women! Fraud charges against Trump ($250 million) – Letitia James, 2022! Joe Man-chi-n advanced from "Judas" to a great man all by himself!!! Our planet won't handle a second term by Trump!!! El Trump receives the honorary title: Man of the Earth = m.earth = merde. What do you call one someone who can destroy an entire world? Satan's executioner (= Bolsonaro)!!!

Germany: 100 billion euros for ammunition – these would be better invested in the rainforest! Bolzo: Brazil's rainforest belongs to the indigenous people! (TV documentary) A trillion-dollar benefit for all of humanity every day!!! Bolzo: Beware the wrath of God and the wrath of men! Putin – El Trump's ruthless henchman! Putin's favorite mind and mentor: Alexander Dugin – a terrible book! His Magnificence Usbeck (Erfurt): Ubi pus ibi evacua – "Where there is pus, there evacuate it" – Gospodin Pustin, (my Lord), you will soon realize what an excellent surgeon Jesus is! You struck Jesus on the cheek – apologize and abdicate! (Your last chance.)

60,000 dead Ukrainian soldiers and 5,937 Russian – they are waiting for you over there!!! If a nuke does get dropped – that would be the end for humanity before 2030!

Putin – are you the cause of the Death Star? Is he what tips the scales? You are a brainless barbarian, a durak (fool), a sore loser (bombing Ukrainian power plants)! Even the dumbest Russian must realize: this is a senseless war!

Russian oligarchs do not care about the people. This monopolistic capitalism has run its course!!!

"Americans! Bury the hatchet at the river's bend!" This book is to be the initial spark for that evolutionary leap!

FET is in the pipeline in 169 countries. God willing and according to Adam Ries (arithmetic master) it will work! (13x13=169,

14x14=196) "Walter, we want to see signs and wonders!" Jesus made the blind see and the lame walk. "Open your eyes – get out of your car seats and TV chairs. Run like you've never run before!"

Al Gore (NPT): "... Until a genius comes and cuts the knot!" The winners of RET are the people here and beyond! Greta Thunberg, a 17-year-old who founded "Fridays for Future," transforms it into "liFe for Future." The question is not whether we can achieve it but whether we even attempt it!

Industrial farming is a beastly affair – we need a "planet health diet"!! Any passionate butcher focuses on quality. The fishing industry needs to reduce its catches by one-third, now! Soon there will be "in vitro fish sticks", market maturity is imminent!!!

Chi-Chi: Rocket "Questions to the Moon", they didn't need to go to all the trouble. All the questions a person could have are answered in the book! Chi-Chi is rebuilding capitalism – F-leap now!

Governments of the world are up to 50% autocrats. NATO has 15 times more armaments than Russia. Do we need self-driving cars and artificial intelligence???

Exactly 598 members of parliament "work" in the German Bundestag – Ex Sonneberga Lux! ("The light comes from Sonneberg!") Luisa Neubauer, FfF-Germany: "... Get moving now, we have the knowledge!" "One came to roll the stone, which was heavier than him, others came, blasted rocks, follow them!"

On October 6, 2011, the announcement was heard on the radio and TV: Nobel Prize for Norwegian Thomas Tranströmer – Haiku – Japanese poem form: three-liners with 5/7/5 = 17 syllables. The goal is to achieve a metaphysical depth, indicated in the image of a moment. "... How the great transformation is to proceed: so far, no one's had an acceptable idea." There are 30,000 Scientists for Future. Now we have the "plan for the planet" (6th Kondratiev), the project "Blue Marble" (primacy of spirit). This is the call to spread the knowledge (initial spark)!!!

Translate the book into 40 languages around the world! May everyone work with all their might wherever God has put them!
So that the evolutionary leap (Forte) may succeed!!
Everyone must know the "Plan for the Planet"!

September 27, 2022
Andreas Walter

BOOK SIX

C A U D A , February 9, 2023

Looking back at August 2020: the Amazon rainforest is burning like never before. 7,766 fires connected to cattle farming! Earth's lungs are on fire – Brazil's rainforest is burning stronger than ever before in history. Animals die in agony, biotopes are destroyed. However, President Bolsonaro dismisses everything as lies. The government still sees the fires primarily as a marketing problem. Many members even question whether humans are causing climate change! Since Bolzo's inauguration, we have witnessed chaos in environmental policy. 20% (!!) of the Pantanal region has already been turned into a graveyard. Another 5% (!!) and the desertification of the rainforest begins (tipping points), triggering more tipping points worldwide – by 2030, Earth becomes a Death Star! Please keep these numbers in mind! How do we get out of this situation?

September 27, 2022
Brazil faces a pivotal election. Former President LULA DA SILVA is challenging incumbent President Bolzo. The two are ideologically opposed. Bolzo refers to his opponent as a criminal and promises a clear victory. According to polls, Lula has 47% of the vote, while Bolzo has 31% in the election on October 2. Similar to El Trump, Bolzo casts doubt about the electoral system. Supporters blatantly call for a military coup in support of Bolzo! His voter base comprises conservative evangelicals, the gun lobby and powerful landowners. To his followers, he is the last bulwark against communism. His opponents, in turn, consider him a proto-fascist. He denied the coronavirus during the pandemic (680,000 deaths). That is why Lula calls his opponent a mass murderer.

76-year-old Lula presents himself as an advocate for environmental protection.

"We will fight deforestation with great seriousness!" Not a single tree will have to be chopped down to plant soy and corn or to raise livestock. Bolzo had joined the Evangelical Church (a third of Brazil's population). This church now rallied for him! ("Satan's Executioner"!!) That is how this church plunged the knife right into Jesus' back! And so Lula, the candidate of the Workers' Party PT, only received 48.43% of the votes, while Bolzo received 43.20%. The nine other candidates lagged far behind.

On October 30, there was to be a runoff for the highest office in Latin America's largest and most important country (156 million eligible voters). Bolzo now pulled out all the stops. The right-wing incumbent's team compared his left-wing challenger Lula to the devil (!) and associated him with a powerful crime syndicate. Lula's campaigners retaliated by portraying the head of state as a cannibal and pedophile. The outcome of the race was wide open! In the runoff, Lula received 50.9% (51%) of the votes and Bolsonaro 49.1%!!! Inauguration: January 1, 2023! That was a close call! Thank you, Lord!!

Bolzo, however, having learned from his role model and friend El Trump (satanic thought incarnate), did not accept the election results and disappeared abroad. He filed a suit with the Brazilian Supreme Court: some of the vote-counting machines had worked incorrectly and so, he claimed, he was the winner of the election! The court shot down Bolzo's attempt. A week after taking office, thousands of people stormed the congressional and Supreme Court buildings as well as President Lula da Silva's seat of government in the government district. Fans of Bolzo were furious and angry about the change. They blatantly called on the armed forces to stage a military coup! Evangelical free churches, conspiracy theorists and gun enthusiasts continue to add fuel to the fire.

Lula now has the opportunity to quell the radical opposition. It remains somewhat inexplicable how Bolzo managed to convince so many people, given his disastrous track record (denying the reality of COVID-19, delivering the Amazon to large landowners). He appealed to the poor and extremely poor. Memories of the attack on the U.S. Capitol in Washington resurface, highlighting the alarming extent of the belligerence exhibited by the new right-wing movements worldwide.

Lula's focus is on the fight against deforestation of the rainforest. Brazil and our planet need a vibrant Amazon. Indigenous peoples take precedence over land ownership by soy farmers and cattle ranchers.

Germany has pledged to promote climate-friendly energy policy: 1.69 billion euros. Germany supports the Environmental Registry: reforestation, protection of indigenous people. An agribusiness company seeks to establish an export harbor for soybeans in violation of Convention 169. Lula recognizes that Brazil can become a powerhouse for sustainable agriculture and a leader in green hydrogen technology. The German government must comprehensively revise the EU-Mercosur trade agreement, as it currently supports feed-grade soy and cheap meat. Mercosur includes Brazil, Argentina, Paraguay, and Uruguay. The world's largest rainforest, covering 7 million square kilometers, is already 20% destroyed, with 25% degradation being a critical tipping point for our planet's climate regulation.

Cauda – news:
Berlin doubles funding for global forest conservation to 2 billion euros. Book "Zieht euch warm an, es wird heiß!" ("Get Ready, It's Going to Get Hot") by TV meteorologist Sven Plöger: "I like to imagine the coronavirus crisis as a tsunami. We're all fixated on the 5-meter wave and don't see that a 500-meter wave on the horizon (climate)". Head of the EU Commission: "... climate-neutral Europe by 2050." "Climate target plan": greenhouse gases 55% below 1990 levels by 2030. 750-billion-euro reconstruction plan following the coronavirus crisis. The number of climate refugees is increasing worldwide (droughts, floods). 87

large-scale fires in the U.S. – Trump denies climate change: "It will start getting cooler!"

27 countries in Europe: Commissioner Ursula von der Leyen, "it's all not enough!" Von der Leyen: "A virus a thousand times smaller than a grain of sand has shown us that our lives hang by a thread." Greta Thunberg, even at the age of 17, diligently presented her famous sign "School Strike for Climate" every Friday. "Biden is reopening doors to climate policy," Luisa Neubauer ("It all depends, however, on Europe, which leads and models the way.") "The European Green Deal – 55% by 2030 – is a very ambitious package," says Ottmar Edenhofer, President of the Potsdam Institute for Climate Impact Research. The price of a ton of coal-based CO_2 emissions is currently supported at $150 globally. The number of dead zones (low oxygen) in the ocean increased from 400 to 700 between 2008 and 2019! (Mostly due to human-induced nitrogen pollution.)

U.S. President Biden puts the threat of global warming back on the agenda (40 government leaders, including China). Experts: "A lot more needs to be done worldwide by 2030!" 2020 was Europe's hottest year. Antonio Guterres – Phase out coal burning by 2030! Climate protest will become more radical, in no way comparable to the coming climate hell. Mojib Latif, in his book "Countdown," criticizes the slow response of humanity to the climate problem and the lack of swift, collective action! Some governments still deny or ignore what's happening. We need to completely rethink/wake up. The CO_2 clock is ticking mercilessly. Ocean health, vital for Earth's life, has been neglected, leading to pollution and overfishing. Every year, 11 million tons of plastic are dumped into the oceans, highlighting the need for meaningful and courageous measures. We have virtually turned the oceans into the planet's toilets! Many people consume more than they need. If everyone lived like the average German, we would require three Earths.

Wind energy generation costs 6 cents per kWh, while nuclear energy costs 38 cents per kWh.

COP27 climate summit, Egypt – without human rights, deceitful climate movement! Protect the rapidly warming Antarctic from krill fishers! Methane is 25 times more harmful to the climate than CO_2, rapid increase observed! The UN calls for a commitment to climate protection by 2030 for the 1.5-degree target! Current CO_2 savings: Warming of the Earth by 2.6 degrees Celsius!! Greta Thunberg: "The Climate Book", 500 pages full of facts (from experts). Researchers declare a "Code Red" for the world with 16 out of 35 parameters exceeding safe levels. Germany has the largest economy in the European Union, with a GDP of 14.5 trillion euros (compared to the U.S. at 23 trillion and China at 17.7 trillion). Can Beijing be taught anything? Early November 2022, the COP27 World Climate Conference: targets defined so far do not suffice or can no longer be achieved!!! COP = "Conference of the Parties", 200 countries. A spirited joint approach is an illusion (Putin's war – mistrust). Jointly set target of 1.5 degrees softened, 600 fossil lobbyists! Risk of "tipping elements" and uncontrollable chain reaction increases. China (largest CO_2 emitter in purely quantitative terms): Neutral by 2060. The world is heading for an increase in temperature well above two degrees Celsius!!! Promised loans to developing countries, annually 100 billion are outstanding! 1/5 electricity (Germany) from lignite – 2.2 pounds CO_2 per kWh (natural gas 0.4 pounds).

Globally: from 1990 to 2015 the richest one percent produced twice the emissions compared to poorer half! Reduce emissions by 90%: lifestyle, efficiency boost, renewables! The narrative of "doing without" is wrong: a climate-friendly lifestyle is a very pleasant life model. Davos, Ursula von der Leyen: "The coming decades will witness a significant transformation in industry." Courage for the agricultural turnaround: 57% agricultural land in Germany produces feed for animals. 12% of the fields – corn for biofuel and biogas! Indoor farming – vegetables in buildings across twelve floors, organic.

Climate adhesive: Article 20a of the German Basic Law – the state has a responsibility for the livelihood of future generations!!!

Cauda – discussion:

Meat imports from the rainforest, soy for pig feed and tropical wood deliveries must be banned. Germany has established a fund of 100 billion euros for ammunition, allowing them to fire for twelve days and has ordered 35 F-35 stealth bombers! Of the 100 billion euros coming from taxpayers' pockets, 17 billion are written off just as interest!

So whose laughing will keep them up at night? Hence the appeal: use this money for the rainforest! Boris Pistorius, the new German defense minister: 50 billion euros per year are not enough for him! One U.S. general: We will be at war with China in two years' time! In two years, the F-leap will have permeated the world, we have no other option!!! Defense budgets must be spent on the environment and FET.

Friedrich Schiller – Ode to Joy: "All men become brothers under your protective wing ..." Chi will then be "the dear friend" of the U.S. and the EU!

A word to Putin (he has already lost 150,000 soldiers and 1,400 tanks):

What are you doing? Is this what denazification of a neighboring state looks like? What happened to freedom, love, faith, and hope? Putin, are you really in favor of the "Death Star"? Your mother will cry till the end of the universe! Putin, apologize and resign. We also want to excite the Russian people for the F-leap!

Putin, what are you afraid of? Your nuclear weapons are enough of an overkill for the entire planet! Wouldn't you much rather work on the "Blue Marble" project than your shitty war (darkest Middle Ages)?

And a word to the wise Chi-Chi:

The "Primacy of the Spirit" is imperative and will come! Your scientists from the world-renowned Confucius Institutes will confirm this! Just imagine: China becomes the leader in the field of immense spiritual energy and free energy technology for the true prosperity of the people. All of this under the guidance of the Communist Party! For a world at peace, for the "Blue Marble" project!

A real FET firecracker for everyone: Water naturally sorts itself on lamellas. A voltage of 70 millivolts builds up. With 10,000 lamellas, this results in a car battery that lets you drive 110 mph for an entire week ... then you have to refill with 4 liters of water! In February 2023, the EU Parliament decided to phase out internal combustion vehicles starting in 2035. The goal is to have 15 million electric cars on the road in Germany by 2030. But only one in four Germans actually want one. Lithium, cobalt, and nickel are very expensive. CATL (China) is now building sodium-ion batteries in Germany. On the exact site that was previously zoned for German photovoltaics, a million jobs have gone to China because of dumping practices ... The automotive industry is the backbone of the German economy (jobs, enormous value creation, material prosperity). The great transition must be completed by 2030! This means that anything that does not run on electricity must (!) run on e-fuels, even if this is not as efficient and cheap. The main thing is that the CO_2 balance is right. The same applies to airplanes and ships!!!

Mr. Habeck, do you really want to botch up/wire up all of Germany? What if the coronal mass ejection occurs? Not a single e-car will then be able to drive nor any garage doors open electrically. China is building only H2 cars for itself. We should also think about a drive system that uses methanol and fuel cells. We absolutely have to proceed on multiple tracks, exhaust every possible option!

What we know: You can drive 6,000 miles on 8 gallons of water, a few aluminum particles and a varied spark plug!!!

The F-leap will mark a shift toward public transportation, conservation, and significant gains in efficiency. What about a neutrino drive or the Turture generator??? What if someone replicates the Pierce Arrow 8 (Nikola Tesla) with a free energy converter? Sadly there's no one in the entire EU Parliament who can ask the Lord when the "real" Tesla is coming. With the assertion of the Primacy of the Spirit, free energy technology will break through across the board!!!

Hey, Habeck, there is a tube: 16.5 inches tall. One megawatt of electricity flows through it constantly – 1/1,000 of a nuclear power plant, I call this tube "VVM". I have also heard of a 14-fold more efficient process of electrolysis, which

uses seawater (green hydrogen). Replace natural gas (heating, cooking) with syngas. (For attentive readers: in the FET chapter it should say: 27 square feet). Mojib Latif ("Countdown" book): end CO_2 emissions by 2030!!! Guterres: 1.5-degree target can only be met by some miracle! Can that be undercut? Masterfully solvable with the "Blue Marble" project!

Davos Economic Summit – plutocratic neo-feudalism, making a killing with coal!

COP27 – Problems cannot be solved in the maximum-profit system – consumer behavior and industrial society must change! Area of agriculture, buildings, transport, industry: use all (!) technical possibilities for greenhouse gas reduction!!!

COP28 is organized under the leadership of an oil sheikh (Emirates). However, these people did not anticipate the F-leap (Plan for the Planet). Excite all citizens, even the conservative ones (e.g., Republicans, USA). Each ton of CO_2 from coal is supported worldwide with 150 euros (perverse)! So anyone who is still voting for the "Alternative for the Dumb" blasphemes God! Great transformation: 100% waste recovery and recycling, (cycle)!

The EU Parliament must be de-slobbed (sticky mud, subsidies). Take big corporations and agricultural barons by the scruff of the neck!

Montreal: UN Biodiversity Summit (1 million of 8 million animal species threatened with extinction, 1/3 of Earth's land severely degraded), 30% land and sea under protection worldwide by 2030 (18% land and 8% sea to date). Funding: $200 billion annually, private and public money. The power of change comes from each individual and can amount to something great. (Environmentally damaging subsidies must be dismantled = $500 billion, counteracting).

One example: EU mass livestock farming and large-scale agri-business are heavily subsidized. Consuming the muscles of dead animals has a long tradition. Now humanity has reached a point threatening its very existence (greenhouse gases). Methane is critical in meeting the 1.5-degree limit. Brutal mass animal husbandry has to be boycotted (cheap products). Lab-grown meat and lab-grown fish must conquer the market (customer comes first). 30 grams of oil have as many calories as 100 grams of meat! Vegetables!! Cut meat and sausage consumption to 1/4! Greatly reduce dairy products!!!

The Montreal Plan is automatically fulfilled by the areas that are freed up!!! SOLEIN (protein powder by microbes), HEALTH DIET FOR THE PLANET!!!

It depends on you(!), your consumption: F-LEAP – a flourishing planet! Then, you can reincarnate 200 times until the next Ice Age (10,000 generations)! For that, "7 years" of "lentil soup daily" – I would do it!!! Come join the "Blue Marble" project! The Plan for the Planet for everyone!!! We want to create a continuous wave of enthusiasm.

Get involved!!!

The last 2 pages are free and can be shared in all variations.

SOLEIN: From nothing – an alternative to protein? Solein is a protein powder that replaces meat, soy, milk, and lentils. The powder is mustard yellow and resembles ground turmeric. It is produced from air, microbes, and solar energy. The objective: Revolutionize global nutrition and protect the climate!!! Already market-ready in Singapore in 2024. Solein is a novel alternative to animal/vegetable protein!!! It contains 70% protein, 10% fiber, 8% fat, minerals, iron. It hardly alters the taste of food!

Production is 20 times more efficient than photosynthesis!!! Commercial production is scheduled to begin next year.

Wake-up call, February 28, 2023

PLANET WITH A FUTURE in nuce (in a nutshell)
SOLUTION: 6th KONDRATIEV IN PROGRESS

Child in the summer: "Earth Resource Day, no more Earth in 20 years!" Grame Maxton: "Change" book, 5 components – collapse in 2050 precisely – human extinction just like dinosaurs ... 2015 Paris Agreement, temperature increase of 1.5 degrees just manageable (1.1 already reached). Documentary: 2-degree increase would be lethal for humanity – 16 tipping points triggered. 3 degree increase by 2050 if we continue as before, actually much earlier than 2050 because of climate change. Extinction of humanity like the dinosaurs. Even worse: deforestation of the rainforest (Amazon), Brazil, by 2030 (worth a trillion dollars a day because of global water supply of humid surfaces), tipping points!!! The end of humankind.

The 6th KONDRATIEV (1st was the invention of the steam engine) is in each case a wave of innovation that decisively advances capitalism.
TOPIC: EDUCATION (KNOWLEDGE); HEALTH (KNOWLEDGE) and ENVIRONMENT (KNOWLEDGE)! In Germany, we are living as if we had three Earths (1.7 worldwide). The FOURIER PRINCIPLE applies: you can only take as much from a pantry as you restock. India and China: We want to reach the prosperity of Europe before we take care of the environment (around 2060). Everything must be moved into a CLOSED CIRCULAR ECONOMY! The BIG TRANSFORMATION to a social, ecological, sustainable market economy is coming with a change in people's awareness. Pursuit of material wealth is over, now health, education, environment, "spiritual wealth". EVOLUTIONARY

LEAP IS IMMINENT. The literature agrees, it must happen. But so far, no one has an acceptable idea of what that might entail. Previous fundamental law STRIVE FOR MAXIMUM PROFIT is "repealed". Higher level: PRIMACY OF SPIRIT (spiritual, global thinking person).

Experiment: a person is hypnotized and tasked with leaving their body, looking at what is in the next room (painter, violinist, judoka), and then returning to report. This experiment succeeds all over the world, is proof: every person has an ETHERIC SOUL, which continues to exist after death (axiom).

DU THESIS FROM 1992/93 (Doctor Universale): GOD EXISTS IN THE FORM OF TREMENDOUS ENERGY and shows up in dynamic numbers! QUINTESSENCE "17" / published as a letter (6 pages of 30 lines) across Germany – great surge of enthusiasm!

2nd letter: "84", APPRECI-EIGHT HUMAN RIGHT 4 (You can do anything on Earth if it doesn't harm anyone else!) Earth is a planet of free will, there is freedom of faith, but KNOWLEDGE COMES BEFORE FAITH: 3rd Basic Spiritual Law: KARMA AND REINCARNATION. Should the Earth become uninhabitable for humans, then 8 billion souls will float around it, all of whom can no longer reincarnate (DEATH STAR). Should the EVOLUTIONARY LEAP succeed by 2030 (CO_2 tax of 69 euros), through Planetary Health Diet and free energy technology – POWER, ELECTRIC, IN ABUNDANCE – everything will be possible, green hydrogen, e-fuels, synthetic gas, EL DORADO (LAND OF GOLD)!

BLUE MARBLE PROJECT – PLAN FOR THE PLANET book "17 and 84, The Godscha of Sonneberg, Free Energy for Everyone", ANDREAS WALTER, 100 PAGES.

The last two pages are copyright-free so copy, photograph, share!!! Please come join the BLUE MARBLE PROJECT!!! INITIAL SPARK FOR HUMANITY'S EVOLUTIONARY LEAP, BREAKTHROUGH: SPIRITUAL ENERGY, FREE ENERGY.

Current path of society: plutocratic neo-feudalism (money rules). VVM tube 16.5 inches, 1 megawatt flows, nightmare for "fossil"!

The magic word is free energy technology, FET!!!

The elites do not have a plan, not for Germany, not for the world. Where are we going to get all the electricity we need? How much does the "Blue Marble" project cost? The hearts and minds of 8 billion people!

HERZ FÜR AUTOREN A HEART FOR AUTHORS À L'ÉCOUTE DES AUTEURS MIA KAPΔIA ΓIA ΣYΓΓ
FÖR FÖRFATTARE UN CORAZÓN POR LOS AUTORES YAZARLARIMIZA GÖNÜL VERELIM S
PER AUTORI ET HJERTE FOR FORFATTERE EEN HART VOOR SCHRIJVERS TEMOS OS AUT
ZÖINKÉRT SERCE DLA AUTORÓW EIN HERZ FÜR AUTOREN A HEART FOR AUTHORS À L'ÉCO
 BCEЙ ДУШОЙ К АВТОРАМ ETT HJÄRTA FÖR FÖRFATTARE Á LA ESCUCHA DE LOS AUTO
ΓIA ΣYΓΓΡΑΦEIΣ UN CUORE PER AUTORI ET HJERTE FOR FORFATTERE EEN
ZÖINKÉRT SERCE DLA AUTORÓW EIN HERZ FÜ
AÇÃO ВСЕЙ ДУШОЙ К АВТОРАМ ETT HJÄRTA FÖ

The author

Andreas Walter was born in 1958 in Sonneberg, a town in southern Thuringia, Germany. He completed his school-leaving exams and military service without any problems. Then he studied medicine for four years in Leipzig and Erfurt but had to drop out due to severe psychological problems. He later resumed his studies, only to ultimately give them up when diagnosed with bipolar disorder. He then worked in the wholesale trade for toys and handicrafts for three more years. Since 1991, he has been receiving a disability pension.

For a long time, Andreas Walter fought against his illness, which had taken him completely by surprise as a young man.

He ultimately came to the realization that he couldn't defeat it and had to learn to live with it. With the writing of his book, he is fulfilling his life's mission. Andreas Walter possesses a remarkable talent for mathematics and is an avid reader. He is single and without children.

novum 📖 PUBLISHER FOR NEW AUTHORS

The publisher

" *He who stops getting better stops being good.*

This is the motto of novum publishing, and our focus is on finding new manuscripts, publishing them and offering long-term support to the authors.
Our publishing house was founded in 1997, and since then it has become THE expert for new authors and has won numerous awards.

Our editorial team will peruse each manuscript within a few weeks free of charge and without obligation.

You will find more information about novum publishing and our books on the internet:

w w w . n o v u m p u b l i s h i n g . c o m